JOSEPH RATZINGER'S
THEOLOGICAL IDEAS

DEDICATION

For the generation behind me, who give me hope,
and to whom I have wished to speak convincingly of a God
who has 'loved you with an everlasting love' (Jeremiah 31:3)

Chariya (1979)
Theresa (1979)
Niall (1980)
Aoife (1981)
Mark (1984)
Ronan (1985)
Luke (1988)
Matthew (1988)
Neil (1989)
David (1990)
Rachel (1990)
Elizabeth (1992)
Claire (1992)

JOSEPH RATZINGER'S THEOLOGICAL IDEAS

Wise Cautions and Legitimate Hopes

James Corkery, S.J.

PAULIST PRESS

New York / Mahwah, NJ

Published (2009) in Ireland by
Dominican Publications
www.dominicanpublications.com
42 Parnell Square
Dublin 1
Ireland

ISBN 978-1-905604-10-4

British Library Cataloguing in Publications Data.
A catalogue record for this book is available
from the British Library.

Published (2009) in North America by
Paulist Press
www.paulistpress.com
997 Macarthur Blvd
Mahwah
NJ 07430
USA

ISBN 978-0-8091-4601-7

Origination by Dominican Publications
Printed in the United States of America

CONTENTS

ACKNOWLEDGEMENTS

My greatest debt of gratitude is owed to Fr Bernard Treacy, O.P., of Dominican Publications, with whom I have worked on this project from the very beginning. At every stage of the journey, he provided what was needed, including contact with the U.S. publishers of the book, Paulist Press. I very much appreciate his and their interest in the project from the outset and their professional expertise in producing such an attractive edition.

I thank the Milltown Institute of Theology and Philosophy in Dublin, from which I was granted sabbatical leave from September 2005 to December 2006. My colleagues kindly took on my teaching during my absence, in particular Dr Joe Egan and Dr Declan Marmion. I am grateful to the Provincial of the Irish Province of the Society of Jesus, Fr John Dardis, for freeing me, during the time of sabbatical, from all responsibilities in the Province. I thank the Jesuit community at Collegio San Roberto Bellarmino in Rome for its warm and generous hospitality from September to December 2005; and I owe great gratitude also to the Gregorian University for the use of its magnificent library. Last, but not least, I thank the Jesuit community and the Department of Religious Studies at the College of the Holy Cross in Worcester, Massachusetts, where I spent the first semester of 2006 as a Visiting International Jesuit Scholar and the second as a visiting lecturer, with the Jesuit community continuing to host me in spite of the fact that they had come to know me in the meantime. Holy Cross – my confreres, my colleagues (in and outside of the Religious Studies Department) and my students – captured my heart and provided an environment in which I was able to complete over half the book that now lies before you. Gratitude is due also to the great professors of philosophy and theology who were my teachers: Gerd Haeffner, S.J., in Munich;

Raymond Moloney, S.J., and Gerard O' Hanlon, S.J., at the Milltown Institute. My postgraduate years (in the late 1980s) were enriched by challenging teachers at The Catholic University of America in Washington DC, among whom Professors Avery Dulles, S.J., John Galvin, David Power, O.M.I., and Elizabeth Johnson, C.S.J., stand out. They were an inspiration then – and continue to be.

Countless others form part of the network that encouraged me during the time of writing: my sisters, Anne and Joan and my brothers, Donal and Padraig; my community at Leinster Road; my colleagues in Milltown; my ever hospitable friends, among whom the O'Higgins's, the McDermotts, all the Littles, the Delaneys, Maeve and Declan, and Lucy and all the Barrys were especially patient with my elusiveness. I thank Sr Catherine, O.C.D., and all my friends at Mount Carmel Monastery, in Zing, Nigeria. In the U.S., I am grateful, in particular, to three families who, each in their distinctive and unnameable ways, have shown me kindness far beyond anything one could expect: Mary, and all the Smedleys, in Laurel, MD; Peadar, and all the Littles, in Keswick, VA; and Al, and all the Campanellas, in Cherry Hill, NJ.

The book is dedicated to the *next* generation of my own and other families mentioned here. Why? To thank you for the light you have brought into my life and to encourage you to go out and share your light with the world.

INTRODUCTION

On April 19, 2005, Joseph Ratzinger was elected Pope and, from that day on, became known to the world as Benedict XVI. He had not been previously unknown, so the reactions to his election were robust – robustly positive and robustly negative. The news hit the airwaves in Dublin at around 5.45 p.m., when I was still in my office at the Milltown Institute of Theology and Philosophy. A colleague tapped on my door and said: 'Come, come; I have a radio in my room.' As we listened, it gradually dawned on me that this election would probably have repercussions in my life. This was because I had completed a doctoral dissertation on the theology of Joseph Ratzinger many years earlier (in 1991); and I had written and spoken a little about him in the intervening years, as well as teaching a postgraduate seminar (every second year) on his theological ideas. Furthermore, I was pretty certain, since I had kept track of his writings – and of writing about him – since finishing my dissertation, that I was the only person in Ireland who had written a doctoral dissertation on his theology. I knew of Professor Vincent Twomey of Maynooth University, who had done his doctorate in Germany under the guidance of Professor Ratzinger. I was aware that he was an expert on his *Doktorvater's* theology, as well as knowing him personally; so I expected that the election would draw him into the limelight also. I was not wrong about the repercussions of the election for both Professor Twomey and myself. Within an hour, the media had found us; and before the evening was over we had already encountered one another twice, in two different television stations.

During the months that followed, various events took place in Ireland, one of which was a public panel discussion at Trinity College Dublin on June 1st, organised by Professor Maureen Junker-

Kenny of the School of Religions and Theology there. Chaired by Professor Nigel Biggar, participants in this event were Professor Vincent Twomey, Professor John D'Arcy May of the Irish School of Ecumenics, Professor Junker-Kenny, and myself. Each of us spoke briefly on a different aspect of Joseph Ratzinger's theology to an audience that included academics, prelates, journalists and students. Questions and comments followed. After the event, I met Father Bernard Treacy, O.P., editor of the well-known journal *Doctrine & Life*, who sowed in my mind the idea that 'you might write something for us.' We subsequently talked, agreeing on four or five articles that would seek to contextualise Professor Ratzinger's theology, to provide something of an overview of how he thinks as a theologian and to look, then, at a number of particular topics on which he had written with vigour and drawn, at times, an equally vigorous response. The number of articles eventually grew to seven, all published in *Doctrine & Life* between February 2006 and November 2007. Two more were written during 2008 – one on Joseph Ratzinger's understanding of Europe, completed in summer 2008, and the other on his understanding of salvation, sent in just before Christmas of the same year. These two chapters are published for the first time in the book that now lies in your hands.

This book is best approached with an awareness of how it came to be; hence my account, just given, of what the German language, with its delightful capacity for creating tongue-twisting compound nouns, would call its *Entstehungsgeschichte*. The original articles – and now all nine chapters – are designed to make the ideas of the theologian Joseph Ratzinger better known and to offer a critical perspective on them. It was this desire to offer a critical perspective, usually by bringing other theological voices into the discussion, that led to several of the chapters becoming longer than those at the beginning of the book. Thus a certain symmetry was lost; but the gain was a greater comprehensiveness. Readers will be aware that, since the papal election in 2005, many of Ratzinger's works have been re-issued, in various translations; some of them have been translated and published for the first time; and countless collections of homilies and speeches, often thematically organised, have appeared also. A number of popular works on the new pope, his life and his thought have also been published. However, a more serious, critical engagement with his theology – of the kind that is not simply adulatory but that provides the sort of critical reflection that he himself invited for his recent book, *Jesus of Nazareth* – is still rather rare, in English especially. Studies are beginning to appear that address this lack of critical engagement with the theology of Joseph Ratzinger, now Pope Benedict XVI. One such is the new book by Thomas P. Rausch, *Pope Benedict XVI: An Introduction to His Theological Vision* (Paulist Press, 2009) which has just arrived on my desk as I complete reading the proofs of this present volume. It is among writings of this respectful, but also critical, vein that I would wish to situate my own contribution.

The origins and character of this book should now be clear, but what is to be said about the path that it traces? I shall try to give a brief indication of this, chapter by chapter. The first chapter traces the emergence of Joseph Ratzinger as a theologian by examining the key early influences in his childhood and youth. This involves looking not only at persons – his family, early teachers, prominent figures – but also at contexts and events: his home-life, his schooling, his time in the German army during World War II, his post-war years in seminary and university. The character of his distinctive theological approach is shown to owe much to these foundational early experiences. The influence of his university professor, Gottlieb Söhngen, who directed him towards – and in his dissertations on – Augustine and Bonaventure reveals itself to be central. Eventually Ratzinger shapes up into becoming 'a professor with an eye for precision and a pastoral touch,'[1] at home within the theological trajectory reaching from Augustine through Bonaventure to the present day and to the company, above all, of theologians of the well-known *Communio* circle. While he has uttered the occasional critical remark about this group of theological thinkers, it is, in terms of contemporary theological companionship, the company in which, nonetheless, he (and his writings) are most frequently to be found.

In the second chapter, since Ratzinger has written on almost every theme of theology, the focus is on distinctive features of his theological work that are detectable in almost all that he has written. I refer to these as 'facial features', thereby suggesting that they allow his theology to be easily recognised and that they also permit the 'family resemblances' of Saints Augustine and Bonaventure, key forefathers of Ratzinger the theologian, to emerge as the genetic strain, if it can be put that way, that allows it to be said of his writings: 'see, he looks just like his forefathers'. The aim of this chapter is to give an overview of how Joseph Ratzinger does theology – and why. The four 'facial features' that are highlighted are not presented as an exhaustive list but they are argued to be consistently detectable throughout his theological *corpus*.

The aim of the third chapter is to illustrate, by taking a key concern of his theology – humanity – how Joseph Ratzinger's actual approach to a particular theological question takes its shape from the influences and 'family resemblances' outlined in the first two chapters. In brief, this chapter attempts to show how he does theology – here theological anthropology – in his context. It attempts also to draw into the discussion at least one other theological approach that poses questions to Ratzinger's anthropology and that highlights the significance, in it, of roads not taken. The significance I have in mind here includes consequences for pastoral life and for lived Christian spirituality.

The fourth chapter is a 'sibling' to its predecessor. Following upon anthropology, it is devoted to the theme of salvation; after all, it is the human that is saved. The chapter seeks to present Joseph Ratzinger's distinctive approach – rooted, of course, in his distinctive theological allegiances outlined earlier – to salvation. This chapter shows how the themes of anthropology and salvation fit together consistently in the theology of Ratzinger and form a very different picture, with their emphasis on 'receiving, not making', to what Ratzinger sees as the understanding of salvation envisaged by the theology of liberation. From here, there begin to emerge the reasons behind the very sharp conflict that has occurred between him and the theologians of liberation. Readers will notice that the method followed is similar to that of the previous chapter:

Ratzinger's ideas are presented, but so are those of an alternative approach in so far as it has both influenced the direction he has taken and can also allow his direction to be looked at from a different point of view. The conflictual or polemical character of his theology will have emerged at this point, setting the stage for what will follow in the subsequent chapters.

Without abandoning its systematic emphasis – and its attempt to synthesise Ratzinger's writings in different areas of systematic theology – the book, in its next four chapters, traces a path that is more historical and that follows, in fact, the theological interests and preoccupations that have marked Joseph Ratzinger's own theological history. 'Disputed questions' (*quaestiones disputatae*) such as the theology of liberation, theological dissent, relativism, and the Christian heritage of Europe that have marked Ratzinger's almost quarter-of-a-century tenure at the Congregation for the Doctrine of the Faith (CDF) are investigated, with other theological voices being drawn into the discussion. The focus remains on Ratzinger's writings as a theologian – these did not cease while he was Prefect of the CDF (1982-2005) – and it will be seen that the thinking of the theologian, inevitably perhaps, left its imprint on the writings of the Prefect. This is something for which there is still evidence today as Joseph Ratzinger exercises the office of universal pastor. An instance that immediately comes to mind, and about which I have written a little elsewhere, is his second encyclical *Spe Salvi* of November 30, 2007.[2]

In the fifth chapter, I home in on two famous theological controversies of Ratzinger's career: that with Walter Kasper regarding Platonism, which the latter found to be prominent in Ratzinger's celebrated 1968 work, *Introduction to Christianity*, and that with Gustavo Gutierrez in relation to liberation/salvation, occasioned by the flowering of liberation theology in the 1970s and 1980s following Gutierrez's celebrated work, *A Theology of Liberation*, first published in Spanish in 1971. Because of the anthropological territory covered in chapter three and the soteriological ground traversed in chapter four readers will have already seen, respectively, the Platonist leanings of Ratzinger and his antipathy to any form of

Marxist influence. The former put him in conflict with Kasper, the latter with (his rather controversial reading of) Gutierrez.

With this chapter, as has been noted, a (fairly seamless) shift begins to take place from a more thematic to a more chronological approach as the controversies of Ratzinger's theological life start to assume a place of prominence in the book's reflections. The reason for incorporating a shift like this is that he is best known for these controversies, and it is useful, therefore, to attend to things well known, having provided background on the theological concerns influencing them.

Having considered two central theological controversies involving Ratzinger and two colleagues of equal stature, the second of which was particularly fraught because the German was by then Prefect of the Congregation for the Doctrine of the Faith and the question of the orthodoxy of the Peruvian's theology was in the air, the matter of dissent emerges so strongly into view that, rather than attempt to deal with the number of 'cases' that occurred while he was Prefect of the CDF, it seemed better – and fairer - to explore his approach to the phenomenon of dissent as such and to try and gain a grasp of his writings on a matter for which, at first glance, he has seemed to have almost zero tolerance. Hence the sixth chapter looks specifically at Ratzinger and theological dissent, a matter which engaged him very much during the 1980s and 1990s and about which he penned some particular, distinctive reflections.

With the seventh chapter, a theme and a time are both very much in focus: the theme is Joseph Ratzinger's preoccupation with relativism and the time, mainly, is 1990 to the present, stretching even into his papacy. When Ratzinger became Pope, his opposition to the relativism of the age was so well known that radio commentators and journalists, with no background in theology, were asking about this relativism. The purpose of this chapter is to outline and critique Ratzinger's writings on relativism, touching, above all, on inter-religious relativism, but also on ecclesiological and moral relativism, all of which are of central concern for him.

In the eighth chapter I turn towards a theme that has always been a concern for Ratzinger: the idea of Europe. This chapter explores not only his understanding of Europe, but the broader question of the culture and values of modern, technologically advanced, pluralist democracies. These are topics on which he has been writing for over thirty years, more or less since he became Archbishop of Munich in 1977. Europe's Christian heritage, he believes, carries obligations and provides orientations that may not simply be ignored. During the first decade of the present century, in a context of increasing European integration and of debate concerning Europe, he has taken up the topic of Europe with renewed energy in many writings and addresses. In the eighth chapter, through a study of Ratzinger's reflections on Europe, some dialogue is attempted also with the thought of other theologians, who have written about Europe as well. This is a lively, ongoing conversation that is only beginning to be reviewed in theological literature.

In the ninth and final chapter of the book, which steers a path between wise caution and legitimate hope in relation to what may be expected, theologically, from Joseph Ratzinger as Benedict XVI, I first examine the conflict between Benedict XVI (supported by others such as Cardinal Camillo Ruini and Archbishop Agostino Marchetto), on the one hand, and Giuseppe Alberigo, Joseph Komonchak and John O'Malley, on the other hand, with regard to the correct manner of interpreting the Second Vatican Council. This is a very important discussion, still ongoing – as the very recent appearance of John O'Malley's book *What Happened at Vatican II* indicates.[3] Furthermore, Ratzinger's point of view in this controversy is significant for looking at how his papacy is likely to unfold. So it is highly relevant in this final chapter, which is focused on the future: on surfacing hopes, wherever these can be detected, while at the same identifying reasons for being cautious in one's optimism, wherever this is realistically indicated. Even as I write, straddling the tension between legitimate hopes and wise cautions seems to be the wisest option as this papacy evolves, sometimes in surprising ways: in perplexing liturgical decisions; in 'gestures of mercy' towards excommunicated bishops of the St Pius X Society, one of whose controversial views on the Holocaust seem to have been poorly researched beforehand; and in (on the more positive side) the Vatican's – with the Pope's endorsement – embracing of the world of modern communications by reaching out to the YouTube generation.

Chapter nine marks the end of the book; but the development of Ratzinger's ideas and of his papacy continues. Readers, I hope, will be stimulated by the book to take an interest in the ongoing journey.

To pre-empt my critics a little, while in no way wishing to steal their thunder, I should say a word about what is not included in the book – and why. Liturgy has not been treated. On this, some work has already been done in English by Eamon Duffy and John Baldovin; and more is under way in German, with volume 11, the first of the sixteen volumes of the collected works of Joseph Ratzinger, published by Herder, having already appeared as *Theologie der Liturgie*. Ecclesiology has not been treated directly in the book, although it is present indirectly in several chapters. The reason for its omission as a specific topic is not only that a fine study has recently appeared in English (see below) but also because there have been several dissertations on it in German, with more promised, and I believe that, to do the topic justice, incorporation of much of that material would have been required – but would have made this book much too long. Such a study probably deserves a book of its own.

Among the ecclesiological dissertations completed since the middle of the 1990s are Kwang-Jin Jeon's *Die Kirche bei Joseph Ratzinger* (Innsbruck, 1994); Paolo Matucelli's *Popolo di Cristo. Origine e natura della Chiesa nella prospettiva storico-sistematica di Joseph Ratzinger* (Regensburg, 1997); Thomas Weiler's *Volk Gottes – Leib Christi. Die Ekklesiologie Joseph Ratzingers und ihr Einfluss auf das Zweite Vatikanische Konzil* (Mainz, 1997); and also Maximilian Heinrich Heim's in Graz, Austria, first published in German in 2004, with a second, revised edition in 2005, the English translation of which has just recently appeared from Ignatius Press entitled *Joseph Ratzinger: Life in the Church and Living Theology: Fundamentals of Ecclesiology with Reference to* Lumen Gentium. A dissertation in English, to be published soon as a book, I believe, was completed in New York in 1997 by James

Massa and is entitled *The Communion Theme in the Writings of Joseph Ratzinger.* It is a Fordham University dissertation that was directed by the recently deceased Professor/Cardinal Avery Dulles, S.J. To date, without doubt, the favoured topic for dissertations on Ratzinger has been ecclesiology, although I have found others also dealing with his eschatology, his fundamental theology, his principles of morality and his hermeneutics. Thus one can expect a flowering of publications – a number of them in English, it is hoped – arising from these studies, above all in ecclesiology, soon enough.

One final point: since this book has its origin in seven articles that were published in 2006 and 2007 (and supplemented by two further chapters written during 2008), the publishers and I agreed that the articles should appear here as they were originally published (apart from minute alterations such as speaking now of 'chapters' rather than 'articles'). To change them because something further has been said (in John O'Malley's book), or has been done (the lifting of the excommunication of the St Pius X Society bishops) is to fail to come to terms with the fact that both Ratzinger himself and the countless theologians and journalists who 'track' him are moving targets, proceeding at such a rate that, as long as they remain alive, no publication can keep entirely abreast of them. Everything in this book has been written during the few short years that have constituted the Ratzinger papacy so far. What I may find tomorrow on YouTube, or what you may find, there or elsewhere, may lead us to rush to the keyboard once again. If that happens, especially in your case, I shall be quite happy. For the purpose of this book has been to make you curious, interested, reflective, argumentative and involved, so that the circle of people who engage with the ideas of Joseph Ratzinger – and with the ideas of those who engage with his ideas – might grow larger and add to critical theological reflection on his voluminous writings.

1

ORIGINS:
A THEOLOGIAN EMERGES

In a couple of issues of the Vatican daily newspaper, *L'Osservatore Romano* in 2006, there was an advertisment for the newspaper itself. And in the centre of this advertisment there was a large picture of the new pope, sitting at his desk and reading *L'Osservatore*.

The room in which he sits is attractive, even interesting: clearly it is not some official office of Benedict XVI, where he receives important people, but rather a kind of den of his own where the shelves are packed – not entirely tidily – with books. To the left, higher up on one of these shelves, are the ten volumes (plus the *Register*) of the famous German *Lexicon for Theology and Church*, a 'must' for any German theology professor and in several volumes of the second edition (1957-1967) of which Joseph Ratzinger himself has articles on subjects that range, literally, from 'creation' to 'eternity'.

Many items on the desk are of a personal nature. I can clearly make out one volume of the two-volume *Festschrift* presented to him for his sixtieth birthday in 1987, entitled *Wisdom of God, Wisdom of the World*. I can see his spectacle-case, a book that looks like a prayer-book with a page-marker protruding from it and a piece of paper under its front cover. Also, there is a *Langenscheidt* dictionary, although I cannot make out in what language (or from which language to which). There are a few other books placed rather precariously behind the leaning *Festschrift*, as well as a small religious picture of some kind and a larger statue, possibly a wood-carving, of some imposing bearded figure that is perhaps Saint Peter, or maybe Moses or the prophet Jeremiah.

The books on the packed shelves are neat enough, but not in the kind of order that suggests they are never touched; and on top of many of them, lying flat, are other, thinner books – just shoved in, really. There is no evidence of any office gadgetry: a pencil-sharpener, a shredder, a laptop, a mobile phone. However, behind the pope, to the left and looking just a little quaint, is a white dial-telephone.

Wisdom of God – Wisdom of the World

Why begin with this picture of Benedict XVI? Well, it shows what he loves; and what one loves is a vital key to who one is. This is where 'Papa Ratzinger' is at home. The elements of this scene sum up much of his life: a life of study, prayer, ecclesial service, writing and speaking, all dominated by an unrelenting passion for truth.

The tranquillity of the scene should not blind one to the fact that this man has lived at the crossroads of controversy and debate. When I first began to study his writings – about twenty years ago – I quickly realized that I needed an extra sheet of paper when reading him because everything that he writes has an element of 'analysis of the present' about it and I needed, for proper understanding, to record that analysis. In all his theological writing, he has an eye to what is going on in the world and to what Christian faith has to say about it. This is no disconnected spiritual writer, but a theologian who comes close to another German-speaking theologian's ideal: the Bible in one hand, the newspaper in the other. In the picture I have described, the newspaper is *L'Osservatore Romano* but, let there be no doubt, it is not the only newspaper that he reads!

It is no accident that the *Festschrift* to which I referred is entitled *Wisdom of God, Wisdom of the World*, because Ratzinger has always brought these two – in his view, generally opposing – wisdoms into vigorous confrontation. As we examine his ideas, we shall quickly observe a constant: that he always begins from the reality of which the faith speaks and seeks to view things through the lens of faith.

He asks: what is the salvation of which the faith speaks?[1] Who is the human being, of whom the faith speaks?[2] What does the faith say about theological pluralism and the unity of faith?[3]

The faith is always his starting-point – frequently because its perspective is seen to be required to counter the false understandings of such things as salvation and humanity that are developing in secular philosophies and ideologies and that do not, in his view, speak the truth about our situation. Christian faith is the truth; and it presents our situation correctly. Passion for this truth, an eye for the world's false wisdoms, confidence that the perspective of the faith can – and must – cut through the perspectives of *this* world all give a critical, controversial, incisive edge to Ratzinger's theological writings in which, repeatedly, the 'wisdom of God' robustly confronts the 'wisdom of the world'. It may not be the case that, in the first months of his papacy, we have heard him speak strongly like this, but recall the 'isms' (or winds of doctrine) that were highlighted for the cardinals in his pre-conclave homily[4] and, indeed, the deserts that were portrayed in his first homily as Pope Benedict XVI.[5]

How did Joseph Ratzinger come to be a theologian of the kind just described, with his polemical bent and his keen eye for where the Gospel and the world diverge? This book attempts to answer that question, tracing his development from the small Bavarian boy born on Easter Saturday 1927 to that man in the picture – priest, professor, pastor (Munich), Prefect and finally Pope – who entered his eightieth year on Easter Sunday, 2006.

Earlier Life-Contexts: Truth and Untruth

Many contexts have shaped Benedict XVI during his life. First and foremost are the people, places and events of his childhood: his family, Bavaria, the rise of the Nazis, the Second World War.

From other writing since he became pope, everyone is now familiar with the basics of his life-story. Much is made of the idyllic Bavarian childhood, idyllic in terms of his experience of the Church's liturgy[6] and the warmth of family life with his parents and brother and sister.

But there were tensions too, and he would have felt them increasingly as he grew older.[7] Due to his father's difficulties with his Nazi superiors as a rural police-commissioner, the family had to move many times, and young Joseph knew four homes in the first ten years of his life. The last of these was on the edges of Traunstein in the archdiocese of Munich-Freising where, on his father's retirement upon reaching his sixtieth year, the family was finally able to settle.

However even this move did not bring tranquillity as the Nazis grew in power, the Second World War broke out, and Joseph was eventually (at the age of 16) drafted. And in the years that followed he experienced much that was profoundly unsettling.

Thus his was a twilight (literally a two-light) childhood and adolescence, in which there existed a communal reality that could be trusted and a communal reality that could clearly not be trusted. The first, of course, was the Church, the second the Nazi authorities. The first was ever more experienced as the guarantor of human freedom, the second, however, as its indisputable enemy. The first embodied the wisdom of God and told the truth about human beings; the second embodied the false wisdom of a destructive ideology that completely effaced the truth about human beings.

Seminary and University:
Definite Emphases Appear

In 1945, Germany in tatters and the war at an end, Joseph Ratzinger entered the seminary of the Munich-Freising archdiocese. His 120 or so companions were a colourful, mixed bunch, many of whom had gone through the whole war, and almost all of whom had served for some part of it, as soldiers. They had experienced horrors and had been marked profoundly by them. Nevertheless, despite the diversity of their experiences and horizons, they shared a great thankfulness that they had been able to return from the abyss and this thankfulness fashioned in them a will to serve Christ and his church and to work for a better Germany, a better world.[8] Ratzinger recalls:

> No one doubted that the church was the place of our hopes. It had been, in spite of many human weaknesses, the counter-pole to the destructive ideology of the brown power-grabbers; it had, with its strength that came from eternity, remained standing in the inferno that had gobbled up the powerful. The words came true: the gates of hell will not prevail. We now knew from looking at them ourselves what 'the gates of hell' were and we could see with our eyes that the house had held on the ground of rock.[9]

This text highlights a foundational experience of the Church that confirms Ratzinger's boyhood intuitions and arms him for life ahead: the Church is the place of truth; in it is found the wisdom of God; and so it will prevail over the evil of this world.

Note his words: 'no one doubted that the Church was the place of our hopes.' Fundamental hope in the Church will remain pivotal for his entire theological journey. That is why he will always start from the faith of the Church, opposing it, indeed, to the pseudo-wisdoms of this world. This method is rooted in his history and leads him at times to too much scepticism regarding the world and too much idealism regarding the Church.

For the idealistic young Bavarian seminarian and his companions in 1945, in the seminary at Freising, the Church was experienced as offering breathing-space, and the seminary provided an opportunity for nourishing their thirst for knowledge and wisdom in a richly humanistic programme of studies. 'One did not want to simply carry on theology in a narrow sense,' Ratzinger says, 'but rather to hear the human being of the day.'[10] So they devoured literature, learned about the new findings of the natural sciences, read some of the 'big names' in philosophy and theology of the day, such as Romano Guardini and Josef Pieper.

Ratzinger read the works of the Munich moral theologian, Theodor Steinbüchel, through which he gained familiarity with the thought of key philosophers of the nineteenth and early twentieth centuries (Heidegger, Jaspers, Nietzsche, Klages, Bergson) and was introduced to the personalism of Ferdinand Ebner and to the works of the great Jewish philosopher, Martin Buber. These thinkers impressed him and he saw that their ideas combined well with those of Augustine, whom he encountered in all the human passion and depth that came through from the text of the *Confessions*.[11]

Augustine – and later – Bonaventure

Augustine is someone to linger with for a moment here, although the next chapter will give more precise attention to him (and Bonaventure) as key figures at the root of Ratzinger's theologising. But already here one sees emerging a preference in Ratzinger's thought for people who write in a more personalist – one could almost say a more 'existentialist' – style rather than for the approach of someone like Aquinas, whose crystalline logic he found too self-enclosed, too impersonal and too complete. He realises that his difficulty gaining access to Aquinas may have had to do with the rather rigid neo-scholastic Thomism put forward by his teacher, Arnold Wilmsen, who seemed, through that system, to have ended up not being a questioner anymore.[12]

But I think there was more than Wilmsen's off-putting influence involved. Neoscholasticism, against which an earlier generation of gifted theologians had also reacted negatively – think only of Rahner and Lonergan – still had enormous prominence in seminaries, although it frequently left students hungry for a more engaged theology. People like Rahner and Lonergan had, in a sense, to get around it; by Ratzinger's time – and in his particular circumstances, as we shall see – it had become possible to avoid it.

Think, for a moment, of the Ratzinger emerging from all that we have been saying: reared among unnerving tensions; attuned to the contrast between the wisdom of faith and the world's wisdom; captivated by literature, personalistic philosophy and Augustine's engaged theological style; warmed in his Catholic heart by the rhythms of the Church's liturgical year. This is a student at once sensitive and questioning, at once drawn to the beauty of faith and repelled by the ugliness he has experienced. It is a young man with a heart attuned to 'dualities' and with an antecedent inclination towards writers with a similar feel for contrast.

Even if he had been fed a nourishing Thomism, I do not think that is where he would have ended up; he has an Augustinian heart, an Augustinian sensibility. Augustine wrote with passion – but so often with a passion that *countered*: countered the Manichees, the Pelagians, the Donatists and, in *The City of God*, countered those who blamed Christians (and their God) for Rome's collapse. Ratzinger writes similarly, and always has. Pick up any text and see how far you need to read before being able to write in the margin: 'enemy sighted'.[13]

Joseph Ratzinger came to write his doctoral dissertation in theology on a theme in Augustine's writings – people of God and house of God – that was assigned to him by Professor Gottlieb Söhngen at Munich University (to which Ratzinger had transferred from the Freising seminary in 1947) and that was initially directed towards an academic prize, which Ratzinger won. This immersion in Augustine was to have a lifelong effect in his writings, in which Augustinian footprints are highly discernible: a preferring of the humility of faith over the pride of philosophy; a defence of the 'city of God' against the powers of the 'earthly city'; and a recognition of the duality that lies deep within human beings who, even when desiring the good, cannot embrace it.

A Theologian Emerges ...

From his earliest experiences – and, as a student, from reading Augustine – Ratzinger has been aware of how much humanity depends on the grace of God and of how much human nature, as manifested in its concrete historical incarnations, is in discontinuity with it. Later, when in his second 'doctorate' (*Habilitationsschrift*), also directed by Söhngen, he writes on the theology of history of Saint Bonaventure rather than, for example, on a theme in Aquinas, there is missed – at least that much can be said – an opportunity to engage with a theology that places greater emphasis on the integrity of created nature and on its 'continuity' – despite vitiation by sin – with the grace that completes and perfects it.

So, there are theological roads taken, and roads not taken; and a direction, a signposted road, emerges for this young theologian's developing mind. His will be a theology less inclined to seek for 'seeds of the Word' or for grace hidden in the human mess of things and more inclined to identify the pollutants that distort and seduce a humanity that is constantly in need of healing and conversion. It will, on the whole, be a theology more attuned to the tensions between what is godly and what is worldly rather than to the harmonies between the two.

There are some concerns to be raised about a theological approach of this kind. It harbours, or at least favours, certain assumptions: that grace flows from the Church to the world, but not really from the world to the Church;[14] that it is better to take decisive corrective action – removing the rotten element at the centre that might destroy the entire crop – rather than to allow wheat and weeds to grow together, to be separated in due time; that the reality of human sinfulness should be in sharp focus from the outset rather than given a less prominent position in a theology that speaks first and foremost of grace as God's gift of self.[15]

The consequences of these kinds of views are – or at least they can easily be – that the 'detective of sin' is more welcomed in Christianity than the 'detective of grace' and that the method of theology should be descending, with the perspective of the faith confronting social and cultural dis-grace rather than searching amid human life and cultures for those traces of the divine that might be *from* God and, indeed, pathways *to* God.[16]

Concluding Remarks

It is time to end this first chapter. It has sought to facilitate understanding of the emergence of a theologian of particular shape and to link that emergence both to his early life-contexts and to personal influences combined with personal inclinations. There has been some limited attention to chronological unfolding, but only in order to highlight elements of 'tensions' experienced by Joseph Ratzinger in his earlier life that have been important in shaping his chosen theological direction. Other tensions will be treated of as the book develops, tensions that proceed the relationship between academic freedom and Church authority and from the pulls between the 'ressourcement' and dialogue-with-the-world approaches that were evident around the Second Vatican Council and its aftermath. If this first chapter sought to provide some insight into how this particular theologian, now Pope Benedict XVI, came to be, the second will attempt to shed light on his theological work as a whole before I delve, in subsequent chapters, into certain centrally significant themes.

2

THE FACIAL FEATURES
OF A THEOLOGICAL *CORPUS*

What is planned for this chapter is a kind of madness – or would be, if some limit were not placed on the endeavour. In fifty years of writing, there is hardly a theological subject on which Joseph Ratzinger has not expounded. Ecclesiological themes abound: liturgy, Eucharist, Petrine primacy, the nature of the Church, episcopal collegiality, the Second Vatican Council, the Church-world relationship, and ecumenism (the list is not exhaustive). Ratzinger's ecclesiological contribution is enormous and spans his entire writing career, from his doctoral dissertation[1] in the 1950s to the present. The deepest influence on it is Saint Augustine, whose christological-sacramental intuitions he drew on to develop what has been characterised repeatedly as a 'eucharistic ecclesiology'.[2]

Eschatology is a major preoccupation. Present in his work are all the traditional themes of individual eschatology, as well as the theology of history and the relationship between salvation history and metaphysics.[3] Faith – and the living of Christian faith in the contemporary world – are frequently-recurring topics; so too is love.

The question of God is richly and repeatedly deliberated. Jesus Christ is a key theme, in Ratzinger's academic and spiritual works, as also are creation, salvation and the nature of humanity. Questions of morality, biblical interpretation and the relationship between faith and philosophy are all present and well probed in his works. So indeed it would be madness to take a 'themes approach' in this chapter, in which I seek to provide a kind of overview of the theological *corpus* of the new pope. In any case, such an approach has already been offered, in scholarly books or substantial articles, by other theological writers.[4]

The metaphor of the face may be helpful instead. For the limit I am placing on this overview is that it would identify *characteristic features* of Ratzinger's theology rather than try to give a full account of the many themes it explores. This limit is feasible because in spite of a common, but rather superficial, perception that there is a discontinuity between the work of the earlier and later Ratzinger, the fact is that his writing exhibits a remarkable consistency over a half century.[5] Thus it is possible to talk of characteristic features, as in the case of distinctive facial features that remain a person's, even as time passes. These features are foundational and mark Ratzinger's theological writing across a range of thematic areas. For example, whether he is writing about faith, or human existence, or salvation, or truth, he always insists, in relation to these, on the priority of receiving over making. For him, the hallmark of Christian existence is that it is first and foremost a receiving existence.[6]

In the emphasis on receiving, it is not difficult to hear the echo of Augustine. Indeed, remaining with the facial metaphor as we explore the characteristic features of Ratzinger's theological *corpus*, it will be possible to highlight, as we proceed, genetic traces, so to speak, of its author's cherished theological forefathers. In a long article on Ratzinger's theology in 1974, Roberto Tura speaks of him as having become ever more a systematic theologian looking through an Augustinian and Bonaventurian lens.[7] In these pages attention will be repeatedly given to the pervasive influence of that lens. In the next chapter, then, I hope to look at what might be called the *fruits*, or at least *a* fruit, of this influence by investigating its effects on Ratzinger's approach to the relationship between the human and the holy.

29

First Feature:
Christianity is True:
The God of Philosophy and of Faith are One

In 1959, at the young age of 32, Joseph Ratzinger received his first university appointment – as professor of fundamental theology at the University of Bonn. As the subject for his inaugural lecture he chose a theologically foundational, ecumenically sensitive topic: the God of faith and the God of the philosophers – a contribution to the problem of natural theology.[8] In his lecture, he juxtaposed two positions: the one from Saint Thomas Aquinas, in which the Christian understanding of God is seen, basically, as elevating and completing, but not destroying, the philosophical idea of God; the other from reformed theologian, Emile Brunner, in which the Christian God, revealed in the Bible as having a name and as being thus personal, addressable, and one, is seen, basically, as running counter to the fundamental tendency of the philosophical idea, which envisages the divine in general, non-personal, absolutist terms.

Ratzinger's solution to the dilemma is to say that the one and the other belong together: the one, personal, addressable, named God of biblical revelation *is* the One, the Absolute of Greek philosophy, the metaphysical One beside whom there is not and cannot be an other. Underneath this lies an Augustinian facial feature: Augustine's refusal to erase the connecting line (the *Bindestrich* or 'dash') between Neo-platonic ontology and Christian faith, knowing that to do so would be to fail to give the radical monotheism of the Bible its most adequate expression.

Ratzinger, in his talk, does not wish to be ungracious to Brunner. But without the Augustinian 'dash', he is convinced, Christianity would lose its claim to be true and to present us with the truth about ourselves that is good, that is salvation. Robbed of this claim, Christianity's relegation to the panoply of the religions in general would not only be assured, but warranted; and Ratzinger has campaigned all his life against such relegation.

That said, there is then an ecumenically sensitive *rapprochement* towards the concerns of Brunner; for Ratzinger is unhesitating in saying that philosophy remains philosophy – itself and other – and that faith, while robustly standing with philosophy in the manner just described, is not at all excused from the work of thoroughly purifying and transforming the statements and ideas of philosophy on which it draws. That work of purifying is a further Augustinian facial feature, one that was in evidence again very recently in the first encyclical, *Deus caritas est*, of Pope Benedict XVI.[9]

The equating of the philosophical concept of God with the God of faith[10] is a pillar of Joseph Ratzinger's theology, and has been throughout his life.[11] It has to do with *truth* – with the fact that, to borrow from Justin Martyr, Christianity is the 'true philosophy'. Christian truth is, in Ratzinger's view, the truth about God and humanity that expresses nothing less than who God and humanity really are. The connecting dash between the metaphysical God, the ground of all being, and the God of Judaeo-Christian revelation, who addresses us in love, as Love, remains in place to ensure the *truth* of Christianity, its being in accordance with what is right about us and about our salvation. This emphasis on truth – of which the Christian faith speaks – will surface repeatedly from Ratzinger's pen as he combats the untruth of ways of thinking about humanity, salvation, Church, etc., that he finds expressed in secular philosophies.

Second Feature:
'In the Beginning': *Logos* before *Ethos*, Receiving before Making

The priority of *logos* over *ethos*, of receiving over making, of being over doing lies at the heart and centre of Joseph Ratzinger's theological synthesis. It follows from what has been said above regarding the unity of the metaphysical God and the biblical God. The God in question 'is the absolute and ultimate source of all being; but this universal principle of creation – the *Logos*, primordial reason – is at the same time a lover with all the passion of true love'.[12]

From this Creator-God, this creative, loving intelligence who stands at the origin of all that is, bringing it to be in love, emerges the assurance for us that we are not the products of blind chance but the creations of a love that wanted us, and knew what he wanted.[13] The divine 'idea' or blueprint according to which we were fashioned ensures our worthwhileness, our character as 'good' (Gen 1:31), our originating from meaning and truth rather than from unchecked forces that delivered us by mere chance. *Logos*, meaning, precedes and shapes us; and we are, accordingly, good as we were created and loved by our Creator. This is creation faith clearly stated, and with unmistakeable Neoplatonic-Augustinian echoes to boot: the 'idea' *human being* preceding actual human beings; the universal before the particular.

I have been talking of the priority of *logos* over *ethos*. There are several other priorities that accompany this one, for example, the invisible over the visible, receiving over making, being over doing. Here we find ourselves at the core of what it is to believe, to make the act of *faith*; for faith is trusting in, and relying on, precisely what we cannot give ourselves: meaning, truth, love.[14] If humanity is God's project (*logos* before *ethos*), then – *pace* all existentialism – essence is before existence and what it is we are as human beings *precedes* who it is we become as historical human beings. In this sense, we are first and foremost receivers and not makers: who we are is much more a gift received than a task achieved.

Not that Ratzinger is denying human freedom, and the importance of human action, here. But freedom is not blind choice; it is normed and guided by what we were created as at the start. The various materialisms (in the beginning was 'matter', not *logos*) are wrong here, envisaging, somehow, the rational emerging from the originally irrational (matter). This view is Pelagian: the rational has to be 'made', for there is no meaning (sense, *Sinn*) at the start. But *making* cannot be prior, Ratzinger says, inviting us to look at how, for what really matters to human beings – affection, love, salvation (ultimately) – we have to rely on *receiving*, because a love 'made' is no love at all (it is just the product of manipulation). From all this it is evident, also, why the *invisible* takes priority over the *visible*.

Furthermore, once again, the facial features of Augustine

are unmistakeable. For he knows from his own life and his own reflections that what is truly important is not makeable but has to be received; also that – here surfaces the Neoplatonism once again – what is invisible, *spiritual*, has marked priority over the visible, the *material*; and therefore that we do not make who we are through what we do but receive who we are from prior creative Love.

The significance of these 'prioritisings' can scarcely be underestimated because they underlie a host of those oppositions that have characterised the theological writings of Ratzinger: his opposition to existentialism, idealism, materialism and positivism.[15]

Third Feature:
The Essentially Paschal Pattern of
Authentic Christian Existence

There is a pattern to the way that Joseph Ratzinger envisages the relationship between the divine and the human – in its many variants: grace and nature, Christ and humanity, even Kingdom of God and history. Always viewing this relationship through a distinctively *theological* lens, he, no less than Saint Augustine, is conscious (despite the 'it is good' that they see as characteristic of us at the level of our creation) first and foremost of humanity's fallenness; and he envisages the pattern of God's dealings with us as being, above all, converting and transformative – indeed ultimately paschal:[16] grace purifies and turns around nature, as does Christ humanity, as does the Kingdom history.

How he sees these pairs as being related is best grasped according to a basic pattern of 'discontinuity', even if – as Augustine did also – Ratzinger does acknowledge that what he often refers to as the 'compass' of nature given to us to steer by has not been placed entirely beyond use by the ravages of sin.[17]

Thus, following this pattern and anchoring it in a fuller theological synthesis, Ratzinger's celebrated book *Introduction to Christianity* presented not so much an *incarnational theology* but rather a newly emphasised *theology of the cross* that, in Walter Kasper's view, deserved further unfolding.[18] It situated conversion, treading the paschal path, receiving a forgiveness we could never bestow on ourselves at the center of the human being's relationship with God. In that book Ratzinger spoke of the cross revealing who God is and who we are: we are beings of untruth; yet an inexhaustible divine love is shown to us.[19]

That is why, as Ratzinger had already grasped with Henri de Lubac, there could be no grace without the cross.[20] And that is why he rejoiced that *Gaudium et spes*, in article 22 (the final article of Part I, Chapter 1), managed to present a corrective to formulations of the earlier *Lumen gentium* that he found too emphatic of human beings' activity – as if we, somehow, were agents of our salvation – and instead placed Christ firmly at the centre and participation in the paschal mystery of cross and resurrection at the heart of human existence, human history, and human salvation.[21]

In all this the 'family resemblances' of Augustine, and indeed Bonaventure, break through: of Augustine, who knew the destruction wrought by sin and the incapacities of fettered humanity to work its own salvation; of Bonaventure, for whom Christ is the centre of all things – of each life and of the life of humanity as a whole.[22]

Fourth Feature: 'But the greatest of these is love' (1 Cor 13:13)

It is no accident that Joseph Ratzinger's book on Bonaventure ends with the above quotation from First Corinthians.[23] Also, in a kind of crescendo text reaching its high point in a summing up of the essence of Christianity, the same words are quoted.[24] The central presence of love is unsurprising. Neither Augustine nor Bonaventure would wish it otherwise. From Ratzinger's earliest to his most recent writing, love is a pivotal focus. His recent, and first, encyclical letter is centred on it. Forty years ago he wrote:

The Christian is one who has love. That is the simple

answer to the question about the essence of Christianity, before which we stand again and which, correctly understood, includes everything.[25]

The words 'correctly understood' are important here, of course; for love is sufficient only when it knows its need of faith, its need to turn to Christ who draws us beyond the deficiencies of our own love by standing in for these through the 'representative' excess of his own abundant love.[26] What guarantees the love that is the basic principle of Christianity is the positively established fact, that we were first loved. In Benedict XVI's first encyclical, it was evident that he saw love as begotten by Love, and as impossible for people unless the Gospel message of love had reached them first. There was, then, a certain realism in the text, even if it left one wondering who exactly were meant by the poor and needy today (refugees?, migrants?, inner-city unemployed workers?, victims of natural disasters?, victims of sexual abuse by priests or others?).

Why not Love and Learning?

I just highlighted the realism about love that is found in *Deus Caritas Est* because I sometimes detect a certain 'spiritualising' in Ratzinger – and in his preferred antecedents Augustine and Bonaventure (especially the latter) – that suggests a disdain for actual history and for human natural capacities.

Take Bonaventure for a moment. He looked forward to the Church in the final age, when the way of life of Saint Francis would triumph. In that age rational theology, speculative science, would no longer be necessary because the *simplex* and *idiota* would supersede the learned and would be much closer to God, because of greater love.[27] The 'spiritualizing', anti-rational, anti-intellectual direction of Bonaventure's theology that is evident here in his looking to the coming age of the Seraphim when contemplative love will be all that matters[28] leaves no doubt as to why he was deemed the seraphic doctor but some nervousness as to why learning will be *replaced* by love, as if the former were somehow incompatible with the latter. Why not love *and* learning?

When Joseph Ratzinger talks of the simple faithful needing protection from the theologically learned, I hear echoes of Bonaventure, albeit in nuanced ways. Ratzinger is not overtly anti-intellectual: but he has sometimes been anti-intellectuals, pointing out that simple believers need protection from the power of intellectuals.[29] That is a line that finds support in both Augustine and Bonaventure. It is also a line that has led to a certain 'spiritualising' in his own writings, coupled with a certain suspicion of the 'natural'; however there will be more on that in the next chapter.

In the remaining chapters, some of the implications of the characteristic facial features of Ratzinger's theology that were presented here will be teased out in a reflective, critical fashion.

It is clear that the first feature, with its very strong emphasis on the *truth* of the Christian faith, underlies some of the difficulties that Joseph Ratzinger has run into in the spheres of inter-religious dialogue and ecumenism. We shall have to consider these. The second facial feature – that *logos* precedes *ethos* – is not without echoes in other contemporary theologians, Monika Hellwig and Walter Kasper, for example. But they seem to have been able to do justice to the priority of *logos* in a manner much less aggressively Platonic, 'descending' and sceptical about praxis than has been the case in Ratzinger's handling of the matter.[30] We shall return to a consideration of the place of praxis in theology in later chapters, especially Chapter 5.

As regards the third facial feature – the essentially paschal pattern of Christian existence – a critical look at the emphases, in this, from Ratzinger's patristic and medieval allegiances will, as promised, be taken.

As for the fourth identified facial feature, the centrality of love, readers will be left to decide for themselves whether Joseph Ratzinger's own words, 'correctly understood', apply to the treatment of love in his theological *corpus*, the characteristic facial features of which should now be a little more familiar.

3

ON BEING HUMAN

In a 1996 interview with journalist Peter Seewald, Cardinal Joseph Ratzinger was asked about his vocation to the priesthood. His response showed that, although from the outset he was drawn in an academic direction, he had had to face the 'crisis' that his vocation to the priesthood was a larger matter and that, in saying Yes to it, his Yes might involve him in the simple tasks of priesthood his whole life long.[1]

As it turned out, things did not happen that way. Still, the incident is important because it reveals that theological work is not an absolute for him. To some extent his actual life confirmed as much, certainly from the age of fifty when he became, first, Archbishop of Munich and, some five years later, Prefect of the Congregation for the Doctrine of the Faith. The cost of these appointments was that, like Augustine, he had to spend time on a variety of tasks that prevented him from devoting his full attention to developing his own theology.[2] So theology did in fact assume a position of relative, but not absolute, importance in his life.

This is consistent, also, with the pastoral concern that marks his writing – particularly his writings on the human being. These are focused on showing to the men and women of his time that the Church's faith is the pathway to genuine humanity.[3] So I turn to them now in an attempt to gain an appreciation of a specific area of his thought, while building, at the same time, on the two previous chapters, the first of which looked at the various influences underlying his thought while the second described the characteristic facial features of his theological *corpus*.

A Dialogical Conception of Humanity

A text of the young Father Ratzinger, published forty years ago, offers a helpful pathway into his theological anthropology. Speaking of how the sacraments are foundational for Christian existence, he wrote: 'first of all, they express the *vertical* dimension of human existence. They point to the call of God, which is the thing that, first and foremost, makes the human being human.'[4]

From the outset, then, we are beings of dialogue: what makes us human is that we are called to be partners of God in a dialogue that begins when we are created and that will never end, because God's memory never fails.[5] Our dialogue with God, in which we are constituted as relational, other-directed, open – after the image of the Trinitarian God, who is relationship, love, and therefore life – becomes human in Christ, in whom God speaks to us as human.[6] Thus the human dialogue with God is not an isolated, vertical, ahistorical affair; rather it occurs through our dialogue with others. It takes place in history, history in which God has spoken to us in his Son. Thus the dialogue occurs in the 'we' of our brothers and sisters in Christ, with whom, together in his Body, we call God Father.[7] Indeed it finds its deepest expression in the actual history of humanity because here, where God-become-human speaks to us in Jesus, we speak also to one another in him.

Ratzinger has spoken all his life of the dialogical and relational character of humanity.[8] Dialogue is at the centre in God's loving work of creating and saving us. This testifies to how 'each person stands in direct relationship with God.'[9] Here is expressed – in historical and personalist terms – what an earlier theology, speaking in 'substantialist' language, had in mind with the term 'soul'.[10] What is being highlighted now is our *eternal* destiny: we are made for God. Therefore programmes directed solely to our *material* well-being will not satisfy our deepest longings. God's breadth is within us; salvation without *divinisation* would betray us; we shall rest only in God. An echo of Augustine is audible here – more, even, than at first glance. For if what we are made for is not ours to give ourselves, then we are, as Ratzinger says (using an image from Augustine) beggars before God, stretching out our hands to *receive* what only God can give.[11] Indeed we are first and foremost *receivers*, not 'do-ers'.[12] But we forget this.

The Dialogue Founders ...

The dialogue that constitutes us as human and in which the memory of God never fails, is not one in which human memory never fails. If the former points to what Ratzinger has termed the vertical dimension of human existence, he is aware that there is a *horizontal* dimension too: *history*, history in which we seek to live out this dialogue in freedom.[13] This history is smudged. In the dialogue, God has not forgotten us; but we have forgotten God. Ratzinger stated recently: 'To a certain extent I am a Platonist. I think that a kind of memory, of recollection of God, is, as it were, etched in man, though it needs to be awakened.'[14] The breath of God is still in us, but oh so hidden!

Human history tells the story of our forgetfulness of God – indeed, ultimately sin is not so much about morality; more deeply, it is about loss of faith in God.[15] For the history we inhabit 'seems, in its chaos, to ensnare the human being, who cannot escape his guilt, who is tied to this history, bound in this chain of the horizontal.'[16]

And ensnared the human being would remain, were this history not broken through by the saving history of the life and death of Jesus Christ, which is at once concrete-historical and, at the same time, if entered into, is able to pull us beyond the prison of the horizontal into a repaired, restored dialogue with our Father, who has never forgotten us. Ratzinger puts it as follows:

> For in Christ the chain of the horizontal that binds us becomes the guide-rope of redemption pulling us to the river-bank of God's eternity.[17]

And it does so when we enter into the concrete-historical life of Jesus Christ by participating in the sacraments of the Church, through which our vertical dimension is re-directed to life.

Already the key traditional themes of Christian anthropology are evident in Ratzinger's reflections: we are nobly created; we are ignobly sinful; we are graciously redeemed; we are nourished back to health through the sacramental life of the Church. However, if the themes are traditional, the imagery is fresh and engaging. Ratzinger's deepest concern is to articulate, afresh, what might make humanity liveable in today's faith-unfriendly world.[18]

He takes pains to analyse what has made the world so hostile to faith-in-God and, in so doing, probes the spirit of our times. The younger Ratzinger tended to characterise this spirit as that of 'technical rationality' – a mentality that is inimical to receiving and letting go, but is emphatic of doing/making. It is, really, an attitude of 'makeability', uncoupled from the truth that we are creatures, first and foremost, not creators, self-makers. Joseph Ratzinger never abandons this highlighting of technical – sometimes called *scientific* rationality – but in more recent times he has added to his characterisation of the spirit of our times the spectre of *relativism*, speaking of the 'relativistic-rationalistic world' that has severed itself from the basic truths about humanity, leaving us trapped in a meaning vacuum that threatens to be deadly, if it is not responded to promptly.[19] He is confident that the human being need not be trapped in a 'hall of mirrors' (*Spiegelkabinett*) of interpretations but can and must seek the real, the reality that lies behind the words and becomes visible in and through them.[20]

The mentality of 'makability' tells us that we must free ourselves from every requirement to receive, from all dependency. We must stand on our own, independent of others and of God. Ratzinger counters: relationlessness is not our truth; cut off from relationships, our truth is denied – and, with it, our freedom – for freedom and truth go together. 'God is not the enemy of our freedom but its ground.'[21] When people deny their creaturliness, seeing it as an imposition from outside, they end up replacing God with a capital 'G' with a whole host of exploitative small 'g' gods, such as commercial forces, greed, public opinion, etc. The tyranny of these is an enslavement far greater. For now who is calling the shots? Our own so-called freedom, our capacity to 'make'? Now we are the victims of our own abilities, of what *we* can do, make, shape. Robbed of anything given that can measure us, we become the measure of ourselves – which is no measure at all. Here the meaning of Genesis 3:3 about how we shall die if we eat the forbidden fruit becomes clear. For to eat of this fruit is to deny one's limitations, to deny one's finitude.

> This means that human beings who deny the limitations imposed on them by good and evil, which are the inner standard of creation, deny the truth. They are living in untruth and in unreality.[22]

A sorry situation is reached: the human being, made for truth, indeed made capable of truth, has now become the being of untruth.[23]

Medicine for the Fracture: Restoring the Truth about Humanity

Uncoupled from its truth, humanity dies: that is Ratzinger's point. When C.S. Lewis considered the occurrence of this uncoupling in the context of human beings' moral responsibilities, he used the phrase 'the abolition of man'. For to abandon truth, no longer to locate the *ought* (*das Sollen*) of morality in the *is*, the *being* (*das Sein*) of the created world, is to abolish humanity, to deliver ourselves up to death.[24] Why? Because as human beings, we receive a dialogical, relational essence and are called to live this in history in an existence that is at once gift and task.

So our true situation is as follows: we have a responsibility to shape our lives, always in fidelity to what we have received as created beings.[25] This means that our dialogue with our Creator is a *genuine* dialogue in which we are neither cut loose in history without a compass to guide us nor so rigidly pre-sketched that we have no freedom of our own. Our freedom is a *normed* freedom – not blind and directionless, but guided by the light of what is given to us with our creation. And our *history* is a struggle between living in line with the 'pull' of this created, relational freedom or else rejecting this 'pull' and striking out, in an attempted independence of all relationships, towards a relationless existence that is, ultimately, a refusal to love.

Augustine's 'two cities' are in the background here. Ratzinger once spoke of how Augustine saw history as a struggle between loving God to the point of sacrificing oneself or loving oneself to the point of sacrificing (that is, denying) God. Attempting, in the mid-1990s, to give this Augustinian idea 'further precision', he said that it was not so much a matter of two competing loves as a struggle between love and not being able to love – indeed refusing to love. He continued:

> This is also, in fact, something we are experiencing again today; when man's independence is pushed to the point where he says: I don't want to love at all, because then I make myself dependent, and that contradicts my freedom.[26]

'And that contradicts my freedom'. Notice the words! Now freedom and the truth that we are made for relationship have completely parted company. Humanity thus conceived is humanity misconceived. Who will restore it to its truth?

Here we reach the heart of Ratzingerian anthropology because, having fallen into an existence that denies our essential relationality – indeed actively chooses against it – we need a strong 'help from outside'[27] to restore us to being our true, relational selves. In short, we need him who is all relationship, all 'exodus', all self-outpouring love. We need Jesus Christ himself who, as the being-of-relation *par excellence*, the 'exemplary' human, can lead us back to love.[28] To look on him, to follow him, is to rejoin the road to our true humanity. Christology, in the final analysis, is the key to anthropology.[29]

The Real Truth about the Human
is in Jesus Christ, the Second Adam

Ratzinger's christology is suffused with the language of 'relation'. Drawing on the christology of John and on the formula *una essentia tres personae* of Trinitarian theology, he reflects on the idea of 'person' as *relatio*, as 'pure relatedness', and shows how all Johannine christological concepts are relational: Son; the One *sent* (*der Gesandte*); the Word. Each of these points to the purely relating or 'act' character of the being of Jesus, who is a being 'from' and a being 'towards', a completely open being that clings to nothing of its own and stands nowhere on its own. The Son is fully open: 'from' the Father, 'for' others. And from his completely open, receiving and self-giving existence, is illumined the Christian's true existence also: what the idea 'human being' intends comes fully to light in him. Christian existence is existence *for*.

With Jesus Christ, the second (or 'last') Adam, the head of a new humanity, a new incarnation begins.[30] He is not some special case of the human being but rather the *exemplary* human being in whom God's intention for humanity fully comes to light.[31] He is the restored image of God,[32] 'the revelation and the beginning of the definitive mode of human existence,'[33] the complete answer to the question 'what is the human being?'[34] In him, the second, the definitive Adam (1 Cor 15:44-48; Col 1:15), we are shown what it really is to be human; and we see that, with creation – the first Adam – a preliminary sketch, a rough draft, was given, which means that we are beings *en route*, not yet ourselves, but transitioning to what we are to become, as this is revealed in the second Adam.[35]

Here suddenly, says Ratzinger, 'the Easter mystery, the mystery of the grain of wheat that has died'[36] appears in our midst, because it is only by entering upon Christ's wheat-grain existence, upon his path of dying and rising, that we will reach the goal revealed in him. The *mysterium paschale*, the life-pattern of the last Adam, must be our life-pattern too; for it is the authentic mode of existence of every human being.[37]

Emerging from the above is the centrality of the *cross* in Christian living. Of the following of Christ, Ratzinger writes: 'Following in his steps from day to day in patient love and suffering we can learn with him what it means to be a human being and to become a human being.'[38] There is a spirituality here: love and suffering; turning round, bearing one's cross. Conversion is *the* fundamental Christian act.[39] 'A man becomes a Christian only by repenting.'[40]

Theological Roots of Ratzinger's Anthropology

I am not the first to notice the centrality of the cross and the paschal pattern of existence in the anthropology of Ratzinger. In a recent reflective piece on the new Pope, his former student, Francis Fiorenza, recalled an early essay by him on nature and grace in which Ratzinger had argued (thus Fiorenza) 'that the focus upon grace perfecting nature should not overlook the cross of Christ and should not neglect that grace also challenges and stands in critique of nature.'[41]

These words testify to what I have been trying to show in this chapter, namely, that Ratzinger's anthropological writings embody a distinctive position, a definite 'take', on the relationship between nature and grace. This position emphasises discontinuity over continuity; it indicates that the way of grace is the way of the cross; it puts the stress on grace *healing* and *transforming* nature (*gratia sanans*) more than on grace *elevating* and *perfecting* nature (*gratia elevans*). In itself, this is unsurprising, given Ratzinger's preference for Augustine and Bonaventure over Aquinas.

In what follows, I wish to trace, to the extent that space permits, at least some of the 'footprints' of Bonaventure in the theological anthropology of Ratzinger. Attention will be paid to Augustine's 'footprints' also, although his influence and ideas have already been uncovered in several of the positions outlined above. And, since Ratzinger was guided, in his dissertations on these two theological giants, by Professor Gottlieb Söhngen of the University of Munich, it will be necessary to pay attention to Söhngen also.

Söhngen influenced Ratzinger significantly, as an early 1960s essay of the latter indicates. In this essay, a *Festschrift* article for Söhn-gen's seventieth birthday and most likely the piece referred to by Fiorenza, Ratzinger points out that Professor Söhngen's writings on the analogy of being and the analogy of faith sought to do justice to Karl Barth's critique of a superficially-held optimism about nature that liked to base itself on Thomas Aquinas's positive concept of nature.[42] Söhngen had attempted to hold fast to the biblically-based seriousness of the Reformed critique, while at the same time not giving up the claim of creation-faith, which Catholic theology expresses in a yes to the ontological dimension.[43] Ratzinger said that he would follow the same basic direction. This would recall – in opposition to a truncated Thomism – that side of scholasti-cism associated probably with the name of Bonaventure more than with any other.[44] From investigating his anthropological writings in the preceding pages, it has been seen that Ratzinger has held to this Bonaventurian direction.[45] Repeatedly he has sought to do justice to the seriousness of sin and the biblical call to repentance, on the one hand, *and* to the fundamental claims of a nuanced, but unabandoned, creation-faith, on the other.

In Ratzinger's *Festschrift* article, he first showed how different understandings of 'nature' existed on the Catholic and Protestant sides; then he sought to move beyond these by probing the original meaning of the axiom *gratia praesupponit naturam*. He looked also at what Scripture had to say about the notions of 'nature' and the 'natural'. Finally, he attempted a few pages of synthesis. In these last, he said that what is truly human (*wahrhaft Menschliche*) of the human being, while completely extinguished in no one, was also unadulteratedly present in nobody, but rather had become 'pasted over by the dirty covering that Pascal once aptly called the 'seconde nature' of the human being'.[46]

This meant that the word 'human' – as languages, both ancient and modern, show – was marked by a two-sidedness of meaning: high and low, noble and puny, or (as Ratzinger expressed it else-where) *grandeur et misère* (Pascal once again). The twilight character of the human has never been lost sight of by him over the years. In a much later work, he says, when talking of the image of God inscribed in us with our creation: 'We see the crust of dirt and filth that has overlaid the image.'[47] So, there is a fidelity to both sin-awareness and creation-faith and, indeed, a deploring of the pastoral consequences that flow from suppressing the topic of sin and repentance in preaching.[48]

A further word is needed regarding Bonaventure's influence on Ratzinger. This has to do not with what sin has done to *historical* nature but rather with how grace is related to *created* nature. The place to look is another Bonaventure essay of Ratzinger's, in which he examines the Franciscan's use of the word 'nature' in connection with an incipient 'becoming independent' (*Verselbständigung*) of metaphysics.[49] There we meet evidence of how Bonaventure falls foul of a fear of ascribing more to nature than it is owed but less to God than is God's due. This leads him to tend towards emptying nature of positive content, reducing it to 'nothing', though his actual intention had been to attempt a celebration of its excellence.

Thus nature falls, so to speak, into a kind of double disregard. As *historical* human nature, radically sullied by sin, it is in need of reversal, transformation. As *created* human nature – because of Bonaventure's inclination to say that all that God has made is, in the end, itself already grace (*hoc totum quod fecit fuit gratia*) – its excellence is eclipsed, even erased.[50]

Bonaventure had a liking for *reductio*, for 'retracing' things back to God; this was a spiritual inclination that led him to view everything, ultimately, as gift, grace. In the sphere of devotion this inclination may be laudatory, but in that of reason it is surely better to try to be correct! As Etienne Gilson, an admirer of Bonaventure, nonetheless once remarked: 'there is nothing pious in being wrong about God.'[51] Gilson reflected, not without irony, on Bonaventure's treatment of human free will. In Bonaventure's view, when unsure about what was to be attributed to nature and what was to be attributed to grace, it was preferable to err on the side of over-attribution to grace, since it would be an offence against piety to under-attribute. However, Etienne Gilson was worried about the logical consequences of such a view and said:

> Since it is pious to lessen the efficacy of free will, it is more pious to lessen it a little more, and to make it utterly powerless should be the highest mark of piety.[52]

Nature, in the hands of Bonaventure, fares poorly, in the end. As *historical*, it demands reversal; as *created*, it is trumped by grace. So it has a tendency to disappear: either through transformation, or through 'dissolution'. Readers will hardly disagree as regards transformation, given all that has been written above. But what of 'dissolution'? Well, Bonaventure emphasises the dependence, indebtedness and nothingness of the human creature.[53]

These emphases have all been found in Ratzinger too: we approach God empty; we rely on receiving, not on anything we bring or do. There is an eclipsing here of the goodness of created nature, a wariness about the human contribution – think only of Ratzinger's legendary nervousness about praxis theologies – and an excessive emphasis on the *divine* side in the divine-human reality that is grace, incarnation, even Church. Ratzinger, like Bonaventure, tends to 'spiritualise' – and to be 'world-wary'. The link from these tendencies to an Augustinian tradition and outlook is discernible.

An observation of Avery Dulles comes to mind here. When reflecting on the Extraordinary Synod of 1985, Dulles (drawing somewhat on the work of Hermann-Joseph Pottmeyer), referred to the presence of two schools of thought at the Synod. He continued:

> The first of these, led by figures such as the German cardinals Ratzinger and Hoeffner, had a markedly supernaturalistic point of view, tending to depict the church as an island of grace in a world given over to sin. This outlook I call neo-Augustinian.[54]

Dulles then spoke of the world, when seen according to this outlook, as 'falling into misery, division, and violence' and as being 'manifestly under the power of the Evil One.'[55] There was (according to the proponents of this outlook) very little possibility of entering into friendship with the world thus experienced – the signs of the times had changed much since Vatican II – and instead the 'Church today must take a sharper stance against the world and seek to arouse the sense of God's holy mystery.'[56] If, earlier, the idea had been that the Church could value the world and even learn from it, now that time had passed; indeed the Church had allowed itself to be 'contaminated' through its openness to the world.

Here again surfaces the Ratzinger call for change, repentance, about-turn. If the condition is contamination, the remedy must be de-contamination, purification. Earlier in this chapter it was seen how Ratzinger, with Augustine, spoke of sin as being, in the final analysis, unbelief: a loss of faith in God. If this is so, then the antidote to sin must be belief: faith in God. But how is faith an antidote? It is an antidote because it purifies, converts. Augustine understands faith as involving purification, *purgatio*; it is *fides purgans*, purifying faith. In Ratzinger's doctoral dissertation, Augustine's extolling of the humble believer over the proud philosopher surfaces repeatedly;[57] and the point is frequently made that it is not proud philosophical insight, but humble, purifying faith that is needed for knowledge of the truth, for knowledge of God.[58]

This purifying faith is a gift from above, not some effort-in-thought from below; and Christ is central to it. It is by him that the human being is purified in the *fides purgans*. Christian purification occurs by means of the eternal *Logos* of the Father – not, however, through the path of philosophical insight, but through faith – because this *Logos* becomes flesh and so the highest purifying to the ultimate spiritual level occurs not through the *intellectus* but in the *fides*.[59]

A number of years after completing his dissertation, Ratzinger was still emphasising – with Augustine and in a certain disparaging of Aquinas – that it is only purified reason, or the pure heart, that can see God and 'that the necessary purification of sight takes place through faith (Acts 15:9) and through love, at all events not as a result of reflection alone and not at all by man's own power.'[60]

The roots of many themes noted in our earlier reflections have become visible in the preceding paragraph. Becoming a Christian means being purified, converted, turned around. The way back to God is through purification by Christ. There is nothing that we can bring to this processs: nothing from the excellence of our rational capacities and nothing from our own powers of action. Indeed, each of these itself needs purifying; and thus purification is the Christian's starting-point or first step. This is undoubtedly Ratzinger's main emphasis. But would it not be more heartening, more encouraging, if it acknowledged – with much greater strength than it does – that we can only be purified by first falling in love with the One who purifies? *Two* biblical perspectives (not one) are needed here: 'the Lord takes delight in his people' *and* 'the pure in heart see God'.

Theological Roots Affect
Spiritual and Pastoral Fruits

The effects, or fruits, of Joseph Ratzinger's Augustinian and Bona-venturian roots can be grasped more adequately if one juxtaposes his anthropology with that of a theologian such as Karl Rahner, who was more Thomist and more friendly towards the world than Ratzinger.

The two theologians clashed. Ratzinger did not accept Rahner's view that, in some fundamental way, being a Christian is not so much being a 'special case' (*ein Sonderfall*) of being human, but rather is a matter of simply being 'man as he is', who, without reservation, accepts his existence, the entire gamut of being human, with all its adventures, absurdities and incomprehensibilities. Rahner's 'anonymous Christian' idea is in the background here, with Rahner seeing as the real non-Christians only those who, in the depths of their living, do not meet their human existence with this reservationlessness. Ratzinger finds himself decidedly unhappy with this approach. How, he wonders, can the Christian be 'really just man as he is?'[61] As Ratzinger sees it, 'man as he is' is the problem, the thing to be risen above, mastered and transcended:

49

Is it not the main point of the faith of both Testaments
that man is what he ought to be only by conversion, that
is, when he ceases to be what he is?[62]

In Rahner's anthropology, 'man as he is' can be affirmed, as
long as he or she is truly 'open', entering wholeheartedly upon
existence with a courageous, unconditional acceptance. In Ratzinger's anthropology 'man as he is' cannot be affirmed until he or
she is turned round, converted, reversed. The sense with Rahner's
'man as he is' is that, if he embraces life, he will be alright. The
sense with Ratzinger's 'man as he is' is that, if he reverses life, he
will be alright.[63]

Turning to implications for spirituality, Rahner's is one of
continuity: the Christian is the human completed. But Ratzinger's
is a spirituality of discontinuity: the Christian is the human turned
round. The sense with Rahner's 'man as he is' is that he can trust
life – and be trusted. The sense with Ratzinger's 'man as he is' is that
he cannot trust life – and is not himself to be trusted. The pastoral
'outflow' from these two contrasting spiritualities will tend to be:
'flight to the world' and 'flight from the world', respectively. The
former will tend to let the wheat and the weeds grow together; the
latter will tend to start with the hoe and the weed-killer. Each theologian is aware of the side that he under-emphasises and (perhaps)
of the effects of his so doing.

Overall, I incline away from the starkness of the Ratzinger
anthropological approach. This may reflect a failure in spiritual
insight on my part, not least about the seriousness of human sinfulness and the depth of our need for repentance. Yet, an excessive
concentration on the need to be changed can miss other things
– and can even cause the stimulus to repentance that comes with
seeing these other things to be missed. For example, what of the
ordinary goodness encountered in everyday life – not only in those
who will one day be saints (Ratzinger's 'simple, humble' believers)
– but also in those who live the drudgery of existence with some
grumbling, to be sure, but mostly with graciousness and, if not quite
with that, certainly with humour and generosity?

The *particularity* of human goodness, its historical, graced, rejoicable-in shape, is not much to the fore in Ratzinger's stark, reversing, radically self-emptying (and rather Balthasarian) anthropology. But need human, graced particularity be so hidden? In John Henry Newman's highlighting of 'distinguishing graces', such as that given to Jacob, the particularity of the receiver is much celebrated, without any diminishing of the graciousness of the divine Giver. Acknowledging that all good people receive, in their measure, the panoply of necessary graces, Newman adds:

> But since time, and circumstances, and their own use of the gift, and their own disposition and character, have much influence on the mode of its manifestation, so it happens, that each good man has his own distinguishing grace, apart from the rest, his own particular hue and fragrance and fashion, as a flower may have.[64]

I find missing, in Joseph Ratzinger's anthropology, a perspective such as this. And its absence seems to me to be a missed opportunity: a missed opportunity to connect with contemporary anthropologies that work with stories: with identity-shaping narratives of selves-over-time that can shed light on God's graced engagement with men and women today. The paradoxical thing is that Augustine, with his own *oh so particular* story, could be the perfect person with whom to set out on such a contemporary anthropological road.

4

UNDERSTANDING SALVATION

Background and Contextual Factors

The most telling objection against Christian faith lies in its historical ineffectiveness. It has not changed the world; at least that is how it seems. All theoretical difficulties weigh almost nothing in the face of this oppressive experience. For with it the central word of Christianity, the message of salvation, remains empty. It remains just a word. If through the faith nothing happens, then everything that it might otherwise say is empty theory, lying beyond verification and falsification and – as such – of no consequence.[1]

These words of Joseph Ratzinger are taken from an essay he published in 1973 in a book that also contained an essay by the German 'political theologian,' Johann Baptist Metz. At that time, he was already concerned that the theological approaches of Metz – and of 'theologian of hope', Jürgen Moltmann – operated with a notion of salvation that placed a kind of secularized hope for the future (*Zukunftshoffnung*) at their centre rather than hope for an eschatological future that had its foundation in God's promise of salvation.[2] Ratzinger's concerns extended also to the theologies of liberation that, in the same decade, arose and flourished in a number of Latin American countries and that – above all in the case of Peru's Gustavo Gutiérrez – seemed to him to place a *utopia*, an imagined immanent salvific state, at the centre of their theological project.[3]

Despite his concerns, however, Ratzinger also had a good deal in common with Metz, Moltmann and Gutiérrez. They had all been born in the latter part of the 1920s. Three of them, Germans, had experienced the horror of the Hitler regime and the ravages of World War II. All four, each in his context, shared a concern about the apparent ineffectiveness of the Christian message of salvation in a world that seemed so 'unsaved.' Ratzinger's difficulties with the other three did not even centre on the emphasis they placed on political and social liberation. But what did put him decidedly at odds with them was their conceiving of salvation (liberation in Latin America) in what he saw to be excessively this-worldly, utopian, indeed Marxist-inspired terms. Ratzinger reacted to this because he saw it as placing salvific agency primarily in the hands of a human history that would usher in the future utopia rather than in the hands of God, the true bringer of salvation. Ratzinger insisted: salvation is not produced – by human history, human effort, or anything else; salvation is received. As God's free gift, and not something that can be made by human beings, it must simply be accepted as that which we (and our world) truly need, but are not at all in a position to bestow upon ourselves.

In addition to the manifestly 'unsaved' character of the world and to the unreliable, yet seductive, character of human historical projects in the face of this, another and more pervasive contextual factor influencing Ratzinger's soteriological reflections was the mentality of the age, which he considered to be inimical to a proper understanding of salvation. This mentality was that of 'makeability' (*Machbarkeit*), the attitude characterising the second phase of modernity (the phase of so-called 'technical rationality') that inflated human capability and suggested that the hoped-for future was ours to shape. Ratzinger's opposition to this mentality was shown in the previous chapter to be central to his anthropological concerns. It should hardly be surprising, then, that it surfaces here also as a key element in his thought about the salvation of humanity.[4]

What Salvation is Not:
The 'Makeable' Future

In a 1960 lexicon article on salvation (*Heil*), the young Ratzinger pointed out that the German language uses two words to translate the Greek word *soteria*.[5] One is *Erlösung* (redemption) and the other is *Heil* (salvation). The former refers more to the negative background – the 'redemption from' aspect – of Christ's action and it became a technical theological term understanding this action rather one-sidedly from the viewpoint of original sin and the doctrine of satisfaction linked to it.[6] The latter never became a real component-part of theological language, thus rendering it scientifically more elusive but leaving it with a more open horizon that allowed the essence of Christ's saving work to be expressed more deeply and less negatively than in classical redemption doctrine.[7] Early Ratzinger showed himself happy with this more open-horizoned term – without discarding what the other term expressed – but fifteen years later, in the middle of the 1970s, he had become unhappy with *Heil*, viewing it as having been hijacked by theologians into a narrowing that was not dissimilar to what had happened earlier to the term *Erlösung* and which now (in 1975) meant that *Heil* had lost meaning for the average consciousness and had become replaced by other terms.[8] These latter were all judged by Ratzinger to be inadequate as synonyms for salvation.[9]

Chief among the new replacement-terms for salvation was the term *Glück* (happiness) with its two related terms, *Hoffnung* (hope) and *Zukunft* (future), as well as the term *Befreiung* (liberation), which had provided its own set of problems for soteriology.[10] Ratzinger concluded that all these terms ended up providing a picture of what salvation is not. He viewed *Glück* as an inadequate replacement for *Heil* because it confined itself to the level of individual happiness, ignoring the dimension of the well-being of everyone;[11] further, it developed in a direction contrary to that of the salvation of the soul, of which the faith speaks, and more in the direction, simply, of happiness in this world now. This led it to acquire a paler, more greedy character: it became focused on limitlessly having and being all that one wanted to have and to be – right now – with notions such as faith's view of the future salvation of the soul being relegated to a side-chamber. This development led to the view that restraints of every kind had to be cast off, for how could one be happy if one lacked the greater good fortune of others, who deserved it no more than oneself? Thus *Glück* metamorphosed into the notion of the full equality of everyone, since only that could really be conceived of as hope (*Hoffnung*).[12] This *Hoffnung*, then, as the full equality of everyone, came to replace *Glück* as the new term for salvation.[13]

To achieve the situation of the complete equality of all, only one path seemed the right one: the alliance of all the disadvantaged.[14] Morality changed with this notion of salvation, now coming to mean 'the task of bringing about the salvation of the world in solidarity with all those deprived of their rights.'[15] Notions of personal happiness could now only appear bourgeois and the real meaning of salvation came to mean, instead, making the new future. Now the important content of salvation was absorbed in the terms *Hoffnung* (hope) and *Zukunft* (future). It is true that these terms de-privatised the notion of salvation embodied in the term *Glück* and restored salvation's (*Heil's*) world-encompasssing intention; however, it is also true that they suppressed the theological content.[16] This is because the future hoped for was no longer an eschatological one, but rather a 'makeable future' (*die machbare Zukunft*) that would be brought about through solidarity with the alliance of all the disadvantaged. Such a future, envisaging a time when there would be complete freedom and equality, is not the eschatological future of which Christian faith speaks but rather an inner-historical set of arrangements that contradicts, in fact, the salvation that is envisaged by the faith. That salvation is God's gift; this salvation is humanly produced.

Joseph Ratzinger robustly opposes the notion of salvation as the makeable future, whether he finds it – and he does – in the political theologies of Europe or in the theologies of liberation of Latin America. However, as much as a decade before his principal writings about liberation theology, he was already emphasising that to see salvation as humanly producible was to reduce it to the level of having, without touching that of being.[17] This was not a Christian understanding of salvation, he pointed out, because true salvation went together with love and meaningfulness – and with human freedom choosing and opening up to these two – and therefore it could never come only 'from outside', from new and improved social conditions, structures, arrangements, or whatever.[18] A salvation that consists in 'having,' that comes 'from outside' alone, that is thought to be the product of structures, that factors out individual freedom, is the target of Ratzinger's strongest criticism, again and again, in four decades of writing; and when he detects theologians buying into such an idea of salvation, he is unsparing of them too.[19]

The most that improved social structures and new increments of freedom can do is improve the conditions whereby redemption might be bestowed; however, they are not redemption, salvation, themselves.[20] Salvation remains God's gift; and we remain dependent upon God for receiving it.

The Salvation of which the Faith Speaks: God's Free Gift

That salvation is above all God's gift is what Ratzinger has in mind when he focuses on the salvation of which the faith speaks.[21] Often – having highlighted understandings that he believes are not consonant with the faith – he embarks on a quest for the viewpoint of 'the faith'; this is his method.[22]

Recently theologian Ferdinand Schumacher shed light on what Ratzinger means by 'the faith'. It refers to a hermeneutical triangle (*Dreieck*) that involves taking into account Sacred Scripture, the Church and dogma.[23] Ratzinger's theological hermeneutic always includes these three in their basic orientation to one another. Thus his theology is ultimately a theology of the word of God, recorded in Scripture, understood in the Church, rendered clear and precise in dogma – and, one must add to be fully true to him

– understood in the following of the Word-made-flesh himself.[24]

As is clear from this last, Joseph Ratzinger never reduces Christian faith to written documents, yet he does consider his practice of going to the written sources of the faith both suitable and sensible when seeking to understand a theological reality (here salvation). This is because faith begins from hearing and the attempt to 'hear' its documents as literally as possible (*möglichst buchstäblich*) is – despite the fact that some might deem it hermeneutically naive – surely not so completely lost in the clouds of hermeneutics that the true identity of the faith cannot disclose itself adequately.[25] As we see, here there is both *fides qua* and *fides quae* and Ratzinger recognises well 'that faith is primarily accessible in its centre (*Mitte*), in which our trust in God, whom we discover in the human face of Jesus of Nazareth, draws us into the circle of Trinitarian love.'[26]

Christian faith, then, is rooted in trustful opening of oneself to Christ and it is grasped more fully through careful attention to what we learn about him from Scripture and tradition and the teaching of the Church.

The Utter Centrality of Jesus Christ

What Ratzinger finds on examining the documents of the faith is that Jesus Christ is the heart and centre of our salvation. If one consults his earliest articles in various lexica and theological dictionaries, one finds Christ standing uniquely at the centre as: the personal form of God's rule, which is salvation;[27] the one mediator uniting God and world;[28] he who alone offers true atonement for sin;[29] and he on whose service of representing us before God the whole body of humanity depends.[30] If one consults Ratzinger's/ Pope Benedict's most recent utterances in various pastoral situations, the same focus on the unique and central place of Christ in salvation is detectable. He speaks of Christ as the apex of the history of salvation.[31]

One of his messages, especially to younger people, since becoming Pope has been that they will lose nothing – on the contrary! – by opening their hearts and their lives to Christ,[32] who is the 'Light of the Nations' and 'the one Redeemer of the human race.'[33] This strong christocentrism is hardly unusual for a Christian theologian! However, two christological emphases are particularly noteworthy. One is Ratzinger's repeated emphasis on the personal character of salvation in Christ; the other is his stress on the universal character of Christian salvation.

Salvation in Christ is personal, brought by One who is Person to persons deeply in need of it. According to Ratzinger, our deepest human problem is God-forgetfulness, lack of faith in God; and our deepest human need is for God's forgiving love.[34]

This was seen in the previous – the anthropological – chapter where I presented his picture of how we have been created for dialogue with God, but that this dialogue has foundered and that God has sent his Son to restore it. This word 'sent' is important: God's Son, the Second Adam, is sent as the real help 'from outside' to do for us what all our human creations (our own helps 'from outside') could never do: bring us back to the heart of the Father.[35] And he does this in the way most helpful of all for creatures who are made for, but have lost our way in, dialogue with God: he faces us personally, looks at us as God through the human face of Jesus his Son. In him, in his life and love-to-the-end, we meet an affirming of us, an ultimate approval (what Ratzinger calls *Gutheissung*) that provides the solid ground upon which our own loves can find their meaningfulness.[36] If such a ground is lacking, if love, which is the unqualified affirmation of the existence of a particular other, is not supported, indeed guaranteed, by an affirmation of the existence of the whole, then the meaningfulness of the particular crumbles.[37]

At this point we see the personal-dialogical and the universal elements of salvation-in-Christ together, as Ratzinger writes:

> In the final analysis, love tumbles into emptiness if there is no truth that is salvation. Human assent, uttering a human 'good' to the existence of the other, remains shallow and tragic if this 'good' is spoken only by the human being, if this 'good' is not objectively true also.[38]

'To be able to experience and to return love is salvation,'[39] Joseph Ratzinger says, but only if there is salvation for the rest of the world too. Salvation is tied not only to love, but also to universality, to truth and to freedom.[40] It is tied to freedom in two senses: in the sense that the meaningfulness that belongs to love can ultimately only be offered to human freedom by God and yet can only be accepted from God in freedom.[41] We are made for dialogue and encounter; and God saves us through dialogue and encounter. At this point Ratzinger's anthropology and soteriology come together: humanity as dialogical is saved by personal face-to-face love, by the love of God made visible in the face of Christ Jesus. We, then, are persons, saved by a Person, saved by this Person's self-outpouring love-to-the-end. Ratzinger (again in words that capture the universal and the personal character of salvation-in-Christ) says:

> The crucified Christ is for the believer the certainty of a universal love that is at the same time totally concrete love for him [*sic*], for all human beings. He is the certainty of a love of God that holds out even to the point of his being killed; of an affirmation that does not deviate one step from the truth – otherwise God would not have had to die – and that nonetheless does not cease in the truth to be absolutely reliable goodness that reaches down into the furthermost limit of being human ('to the end', Jn 13:1). The crucified Christ is the concrete affirmation of God that is valid for every human being and that makes him (*sic*) certain that he, the human being, is taken so utterly seriously by God that God does not permit that this ('serious case' [*Ernstfall*] of the human) would spare him his own deathly fate. Being taken seriously belongs to being affirmed. The crucified God is the (ultimate) test-case of the affirmation ('it is good') of the final day of creation. The cross says this: there is a truth about the human that is good and kindly – that is his salvation.[42]

The Content of the Salvation Received in Christ

Through God's gift of salvation we receive: forgiveness, through Christ, for sin; a share in the 'for'-existence of God-made-human; and a promise that we shall rise with Christ to eternal life with God.[43] Ratzinger keeps this (unmakeable) content of salvation in focus by reminding us that christology has two basic points (*Konstruktionspunkte*), one located in the past, the other in the future. The former is articulated in the traditional doctrine of original sin, the latter in the biblical idea of the 'second' or 'last' Adam who (as was seen in the previous chapter) reveals to and begins for us the definitive way of being human.[44]

Note the word 'definitive.' Already in Christ we are called into a future that is at once historical and eschatological.[45] This becomes even clearer when the resurrection enters the picture: 'To believe in the Resurrection of Jesus means ... to believe in the *eschaton* in history, in the historicity of God's eschatological action.'[46] Salvation-in-Christ, then, touches all of history: past, present and future. The second construction point of christology assures this embrace of the entirety of history because it means 'that God conquers man's past – conquers sin – by calling him into the future – into Christ.'[47] And in Christ, salvation is present now: 'Salvation is Person; everywhere that Christ (and through him God) reigns, there is salvation.'[48]

Ratzinger's first christological construction-point leads him to state, repeatedly, that salvation is primarily salvation from sin.[49] Precisely as this, since the fundamental characteristic of sin is lack of faith in God (Augustine), the gift of God's forgiveness, even now, restores us to relationship with God's own self and with one another.

The key agent here is God. Sinners have to rely on receiving, on accepting with outstretched hands the gift of being turned round, of being converted. Conversion – *metanoia* – is the fundamental Christian act.[50] Our old existence is taken away and a new one is received: we are drawn beyond the isolation of the 'I' into the 'we' of the believing community.[51] This is a move – or rather, a being moved – away from egoism and preoccupation with self into the relational 'we' that is our true character and destiny. The sacrament of baptism's imagery of passing from death to new life captures it very well; for there is death to the old self and birth to new life.[52] The mystery of the wheat-grain (Jn 12: 24-25) is here; life is found in death. In an example lacking somewhat in mutuality, Ratzinger likens it to the wife's renunciation of her own, and adoption of her husband's, name in marriage: she lets go – there is a 'death' – for the sake of the new life that love brings (in fairness, he does add that 'this surrender of the old is, for both spouses, the condition of the new that is opening to them'). What is central here is that a new existence, a 'we'-existence, an ecclesial existence, is received when a person (he has adults in mind) chooses baptism and joins the community of salvation.[53]

Receiving forgiveness and a new existence means being 'done unto;' it means taking from Another what we need but are powerless to give ourselves. In this taking we accept, we allow ourselves to be 'done unto.' Here Ratzinger subtly balances the delicate tension between gift and task, *Gabe und Aufgabe*, highlighting the fundamental gift-character of the *metanoia* that we receive (*Gabe*) but without overlooking our own involvement in the process of receiving it (*Aufgabe*).[54] This involvement has to do, not so much with changes that we make but rather with changes that we permit to be made to us, thus not hindering the effects of the gift received.[55] These effects are real, conferring a freedom from and a freedom for. We are freed from 'going it alone,' from egoism, from proud self-sufficiency; and the pride of our unbelief is replaced by the humility of faith.[56] And so we are shaped for receiving that new existence in which we are made sons and daughters of God and sharers in the 'for-existence' of the Son himself.[57]

To receive such an existence is what theology refers to as divinization. This notion is central to Ratzinger's understanding of salvation in Christ. Christians, he says, are incorporated into Christ; indeed, salvation consists in becoming 'the body of Christ,' that is, in becoming 'like Christ himself.'[58] Traces of Joseph Ratzinger's eucharistic ecclesiology are surfacing here: in the Eucharist Christians become one with each other in the one Body of the Lord.[59] To become one with him (and others) in this way is to become like him, to grow into him who was from God and for others; this is the gift of divinization.

Recalling here Ratzinger's second christological construction point, located in the future, it becomes evident what Christians are called towards: they are invited to the 'being for' of Christ, the Second Adam, in whose 'existence for' the shape of their own divinized existence is truly disclosed. This gift of divinization brings about a real participation in him that can make a genuine difference both to one's own existence and to that of the world.[60] For just as Christ, who is the 'representative' of the whole of humanity before God, is the *one* who 'stands in' for all, so Christians (the Church), in faithful discipleship of him, participating in his existence-for, become the *few* for the *many*, thus serving the world with a love that – because it is linked to Christ's sufficient love – makes a contribution to all.[61]

Being divinized, then, is a gift not only for oneself but also for others. Ratzinger conceives of it as being both ontological and historical. It involves a genuine participation in the love of Christ, a participation in which we can grow, so that God's salvation is made present and real in human history.[62] And so believers are brought into the movement whereby creatures return to God. Realizing divinization in history is the carrying out of God's will and it is an activity that we at once receive as a gift (*Gabe*), yet exercise as a task (*Aufgabe*). This reality of being divinized is humanity's salvific truth. A salvation conceived in lesser terms would fall short of that yearning for freedom that characterises humanity today (a point made by Ratzinger over thirty years ago in *Doctrine & Life* when opposing Hans Küng's preference for speaking of 'humanization' rather than 'divinization').[63]

As well as forgiveness of sin and incorporation into the 'for-existence' of Jesus, Christian salvation contains another – indeed the greatest – gift of all: resurrection from the dead. Joseph Ratzinger states this belief succinctly: 'The Christian hopes for the resurrection of the dead.'[64] Beginning with a reflection on the fifteenth chapter of St Paul's First Letter to the Corinthians and going on to probe how the dogma of resurrection has unfolded in history – in other words, following his method of examining that resurrection of which 'the faith' speaks – he says (with St Paul) that Christian faith and preaching are senseless without the hope of resurrection, which includes the expectation of a new heaven and a new earth, that is, the conviction that the whole of history – indeed the entire cosmos – will prove ultimately meaningful and intelligible. It also includes the fulfilment of the individual in a life that continues beyond the grave. However, it does *not* include the expectation of an inner-worldly state of definitive well-being; this last is not a Christian notion, even if the idea of progress actually did develop from within Christianity.[65]

With these three characteristics of Christian faith in the resurrection, Ratzinger, as well as stating this faith positively, has managed also, first, to oppose spiritualising, un-bodily, unworldly interpretations of resurrection; second, to insist upon individual fulfilment after death against those who would empty out of salvation the idea of the 'salvation of the soul,' an idea that he – not at all uncontroversially – makes central in his eschatological writing;[66] and third, to reject notions of salvation, and the theologies supporting them, that he views as placing projects for history at their core. As always with Ratzinger's theological writing, one needs to be aware not only of what he is saying but also of whom he has in mind when saying it. It will be necessary to attend to this point again shortly.

Lest his rejection of promises for history – and the energy that these produce – would leave him vulnerable to the Marxist critique that he encourages people to look heavenward while ignoring the ills of the earth, Joseph Ratzinger insists that salvation as the promise of resurrection and eternal life should not distract people from their earthly responsibilities and tasks but rather provide them with new motives and energy to embrace them.[67] Anyone who is confronted with the message of resurrection 'must start running. It sets him in motion because it is important that it should spread farther before it is too late.'[68]

In this sense, we note that for Ratzinger – in a manner that would not disappoint his Lutheran colleagues (who have always been close at hand, certainly in his professorial years) – good works are understood to 'flow' from faith.[69] This is consistent with Ratzinger's fourth thesis in his 1973 article about how universal love (salvation) can call forth particular love, giving it a meaning and sufficiency that it could never have without the 'it is true' of Christ's sufficient saving love.[70] Salvation is found, then, in love; but it is love made sufficient by faith; it is faith that makes it possible. There is ecumenical sensitivity here: without faith there is no salvation. Nonetheless there is also difference from Luther in that love, made sufficient by Jesus' perfect love-to-the-end, is not then entirely excluded from salvation. However it is present there not as a 'work' in the profane sense (that would be deserving of the censure of Luther: '*maledicta sit caritas*'[71]) but rather as a gift of God within the saving process.

Some Critical Reflections

The emphases in Ratzinger's approach to salvation parallel, not surprisingly, those characteristics of his theology of the human being that were highlighted in the previous chapter. His focus on the 'unmakeability' of salvation corresponds with his view of human beings as first and foremost receivers; and his rejection of *praxis*-theologies as shifting the agency in salvation from God to history (and to human historical projects) expresses this anti-makeability stance.[72] His insistence that salvation is primarily salvation from sin is consistent with his view that the first step for the Christian is to turn around – to be converted – because his/her state is fallenness (*Verfallenheit*).[73]

This is also consistent with his understanding of the nature-grace relationship more in terms of *discontinuity* than of continuity, an understanding influenced, as was seen in the last chapter, by his allegiances in theology to Augustine (and Bonaventure), and parallelled in his soteriology by a perception that human activity in the world tends to be more discontinuous than continuous with the values of Christ's Kingdom.[74] Overall, then, just as in his anthropology, so too in Ratzinger's soteriology are there distinctive emphases; and there remains his characteristic stance on the relationship between the human and the divine (human activity and salvation). This stance is present in a fairly seamless way through the domains of anthropology and soteriology.

I would like to make just a single observation in relation to it. Here it is necessary to return to a point made a little earlier about it being important to attend not only to what Ratzinger is saying but also to whom he is saying it. In his 1973 article raising preliminary questions for a theology of redemption, we find him – at one point drawing on the work of Joseph Pieper – in the dialogical-personalist framework that has been seen to characterise so much of his thinking about human beings. Within this framework, having noted, with Pieper, that the core of love is an unconditional affirmation (*Gutheissung*) that receives the guarantee of its unconditionality from a *Gutheissung* that it cannot bestow upon itself, Ratzinger goes on to speak about 'fragments of salvation' (*Heilsfragmente*) that are not themselves salvation *becoming* salvation, once they are touched by the unconditional divine *Gutheissung*.[75] In this framework, then, of interpersonal human love, he is able to speak of the presence of salvation – albeit not the entirety of salvation. That is because this human love is *made* sufficient by what God gives to it in faith. And so it is enabled to acquire salvific significance – as was seen above, in Ratzinger's nuanced position *vis à vis* a Lutheran approach.

Outside of his dialogical-personalist framework, however, matters are different. In the *social* sphere, for example, when liberation and political theologians are in his sights, Ratzinger rejects any talk of 'fragments of salvation,' much less of salvation itself. Whenever he speaks of social structures, for example, or of good social conditions that have their roots in the decisions of good persons, while not denying their helpfulness, he never uses the language of 'fragments of salvation' with regard to them and he certainly avoids the world 'salvation' itself.[76] His preferred words, which have almost become a refrain, are that in such social circumstances we do not have 'redemption', but, at best, an opening up of conditions for receiving redemption.[77]

Ratzinger's exchanges with liberation theologian Gustavo Gutiérrez in the mid-1980s illustrate this matter lucidly. An element of their dispute (about which more in the next chapter) concerned the relationship between temporal progress (or 'liberation') and the growth of Christ's Kingdom (or 'salvation'). A text of the Vatican II Pastoral Constitution, *Gaudium et Spes*, which sought to express itself on exactly this topic and which went through no fewer than five major drafts, is central. It is paragraph 39; and the final statement reached was a compromise – a weak statement really – announcing that the one (earthly progress) is 'of vital concern' to the other (the Kingdom of God).[78] Ratzinger took this in the direction of emphasising what the sentence preceding it had said concerning how 'earthly progress must be carefully distinguished from the growth of Christ's kingdom,' adding that the two 'do not belong to the same order.'[79] Gutiérrez found the *Gaudium et Spes* formulation inadequate and saw in its open unfinished nature a leaving open, by the Council, of the matter of how subsequent theology should interpret the liberation-salvation relationship; and so he made a suggestion.[80]

Gutiérrez suggests that salvation, the growth of Christ's Kingdom, can be thought of as being present in temporal progress, or liberation, although not completely present. The two are distinct; but the distinction between them should be seen not in static terms, but from a dynamic viewpoint: in earthly liberations, the Kingdom of God is present; but it is not completely present, liberation is not all of salvation. Gutiérrez says: 'the historical, political liberating event is the growth of the Kingdom and is a salvific event; but it is not *the* coming of the Kingdom, not all of salvation.'[81] This position of Gutiérrez exceeds Ratzinger's words about human achievements at best opening up conditions for redeemed existence, while not being redemption themselves. But it does not much exceed what Ratzinger says, within his dialogical-personalist framework, when he points to 'fragments of salvation' being detectable in human interpersonal love even before God's salvific affirmation (*Gutheissung*) provides for these fragments the trustworthy foundation that they need in order for them to become salvation itself.[82]

When Ratzinger speaks from within a framework more congenial to his own way of thinking, he is much nearer to Gutiérrez and much less cautious about speaking of at least traces of salvation in the human world. However, when he enters the social framework, the preferred space of Gutiérrez and the theologians of liberation, he disallows the finding of salvation, even fragmentarily, in liberations that are achieved. But why exactly? Is he not being somewhat inconsistent here? For these liberations can have a claim to being fragmentarily salvific in a manner similar to love between two persons if they are born of persons working together, in freedom and in love, for the good of their fellow human beings. Furthermore, if the partial liberations that they represent receive, in faith, that affirmation (*Gutheissung*) that is God's 'yes' to the whole, God's promise of a new heavens and a new earth, then might this not be seen – analogously to the divine *Gutheissung* that situates the affirmation of the other in the context of God's yes to every person – as the converting of fragments of salvation into salvation itself (although not, of course, full eschatological salvation)?

Were Ratzinger to see traces of salvation like this in the context of human social relationships it would bring his position closer to what it is in the dialogical-personalist sphere; what, then, holds him back? Maybe it is that he thinks the argument that earthly liberations, good social structures and just laws can embody salvation, be salvific, equates to the materialist position that structures will make people good. He is right in rejecting that; but that is not being said here. What is being said is this: not only is love between individuals good, a salvific fragment, capable of being raised in faith to salvation itself, but so also is the love of a group of persons who act on behalf of oppressed people good, a salvific fragment, capable of being raised in faith to salvation itself – precisely because it is a response of these persons together to grace, which in turn leads them to act together for the unliberated and to achieve, under this same grace and not outside of it, a partial liberation for them. To limit redemption and grace to the intrapersonal and interpersonal spheres is to narrow the embrace of the axiom that 'grace builds on nature'; for it is our nature to be social as well as to be individual and interpersonal.

What is wrong with such nuanced talking about salvation in the social sphere? Its exclusion is excessive and causes Ratzinger to shortchange his own anthropology. Talking to liberationists, he becomes a bit like Luther polemicising against works, consigning all striving for liberation to the sphere of the profane. Yet talking with Lutherans in mind, he finds space for what human beings do to be salvific – once it is made sufficient through faith. His interlocutors are decisive for his positions. I shall revisit the Ratzinger-Gutiérrez exchange in the next chapter.

5

QUAESTIONES DISPUTATAE: WITH WALTER KASPER AND GUSTAVO GUTIÉRREZ

In the life of Joseph Ratzinger, both as professor and as cardinal-prefect, there lies a history of dispute that calls for some exploration if an adequate window on his theological impact is to be provided in this book. Accordingly, this chapter and the next will be devoted to a consideration of some of the memorable *quaestiones disputatae* that have marked his life. As I write, a new controversy is raging, this time over a quotation included in an address he gave at the University of Regensburg. I shall touch on that in a later chapter, which will focus on disputed questions in ecumenism and inter-religious dialogue. But, first, some earlier disputes.

Here I home in on two famous controversies: that with Walter Kasper concerning Platonism, occasioned by Ratzinger's 1968 book, *Introduction to Christianity*; and, in the 1980s, his dispute with liberation theology.

First Dispute:
With Walter Kasper,
concerning Ratzinger's 'Platonism'

This sharp exchange occurred in the late 1960s when Ratzinger was at Tübingen and Kasper was at Münster (though soon to arrive at Tübingen). The occasion was the publication of Ratzinger's *Introduction to Christianity*. Kasper wrote a robust review.[1] Ratzinger responded energetically.[2] Kasper then responded to the response;[3] and Ratzinger appended a concluding word following that second response of Kasper.[4]

In Kasper's appreciative but critical review, he homed in on the Platonism that he found to permeate the theological synthesis offered in the book. Ratzinger's starting-point, he noted, was the Platonic dialectic between the world of the senses and the world 'above the senses'.[5] Ratzinger held that the human being lived in the realm of what was visible and tangible, but that he or she did seek meaning – and that such meaning could be guaranteed only by what was invisible. Indeed, faith meant the option for the primacy of the invisible over the visible. The invisible was the truly real, providing the ground and possibility for reality as a whole.[6]

Kasper questioned Ratzinger's starting with the Platonic dialectic *visible/invisible*. He proposed an alternative: a histori-cally-oriented theology, starting from the human being's concrete interwovenness with nature, society, culture and history. Different theological consequences would flow from such a starting point, he said. The meaning that we seek would then be mediated to us only through our concrete, historical encountering of the world and of people, or else not at all; and the result would be a far greater taking seriously of the concrete problems of people.[7]

A text not quoted by Kasper (although it occurs just after Ratzinger's remarks on the primacy of the invisible) confirms the Platonic character of Ratzinger's work:

> Man's natural centre of gravity draws him to the visible, to what he can take in his hand and hold as his own. He has to turn round inwardly in order to see how badly he is neglecting his own interests by letting himself be drawn along in this way by his natural centre of gravity. He must turn round to recognize how blind he is if he trusts only what he sees with his eyes. Without this change of direction, without this resistance to the natural centre of gravity, there can be no belief.[8]

This is a telling text. In its own way (*pace* Kasper), it *is* concrete-historical, but the concrete-historical focus of Ratzinger is not Kasper's human being interwoven with nature, culture, and so on, but rather sullied human nature – what humans have become through sin. Echoes of Plato's cave resound: we human beings live in blindness and we must turn around if we are to see the truth. Plato's conversion from shadow to reality and the Christian's from the visible to the invisible (recall also Augustine) dovetail.

Ratzinger starts from human beings in need of change; Kasper suggests starting from human beings' concrete historical situatedness – and seeking the mediation of the divine, the invisible, in and through it. For Ratzinger, to encounter God we must *turn* around; for Kasper, to encounter God we must *look* around. The consequences of the Platonic-Ratzingerian position are severe in relation to praxis; for we begin by turning *from* the world, not *to* it. The consequences of Kasper's position are that praxis is truly central: Christianity, Kasper points out, is concerned with *doing the truth* (Jn 3:21).[9]

Kasper argues that Ratzinger's founding his work on the Platonic dialectic of *visible/invisible* sheds light on his treatment of a variety of theological positions (too numerous to pursue here). It also, and most seriously of all, ultimately causes him to end up – unwittingly, largely, and even unwillingly – espousing a principle of idealism that in fact he would prefer to reject, this principle being the identity of freedom and necessity.[10] He falls into espousing this, Kasper points out, when he combines his Platonic starting-point (*visible/invisible*) with his view that human beings only reach God by being with *others* and by receiving themselves as a gift of love. Christian faith is thus not some speculative conception, in Ratzinger's view; rather it rests on that which comes to us as something positive, something that we receive (note the same emphasis as always: *received* not *made*, not from our doing).[11] Ratzinger states:

> It seems to me that from here the squaring of the theological circle, so to speak, can be accomplished; that the intrinsic necessity of the apparently historical contin-

gency of Christianity can be shown, the 'must' of its – to us – objectionable positivity as an event that comes to us from outside. The antithesis, so heavily emphasised by Lessing, between *vérité de fait* (contingent factual truth) and *vérité de raison* (necessary intellectual truth) here becomes surmountable. The contingent, the external is what is necessary to man; only in the arrival of something from outside does he open up inwardly. God's disguise as man in history 'must' be – with the necessity of freedom.[12]

Now that, says Kasper, is idealism, whether one wishes it or not! Schelling and Hegel, who themselves were concerned to demonstrate the historically contingent to be the necessary – and thereby to establish the identity of freedom and necessity – would have been happy with it.[13] Ratzinger may well intend to present and to emphasise the 'positivity' of Christianity (rather than to assert a kind of 'deducibility,' or 'necessity' for it), but his intentions clash with (*widerstreiten*) the immanent logic of his categories and arguments.[14]

Ratzinger reports himself perplexed by Kasper's charges of Platonism: 'I have to admit that, in spite of thoroughgoing reflection, these theses have in large measure remained incomprehensible to me.'[15] He denies them. But he does not deny that there exists a lasting truth that we humans *receive*. If his acceptance of this position, which the movement *Kritischer Katholizismus* (mentioned also by Kasper) does consider to be Platonism, makes him a Platonist, then he is one – and willingly.[16]

With regard to 'the horizon of a historical thinking' that was pointed to by Kasper as the correct solution for his undertaking, Ratzinger reports that it remains completely hazy (*verschwommen*) to him, in so far as what Kasper means is not just a repeating of what is generally known. Then he adds: 'perhaps the word "historical" should be forbidden completely to theologians for a while, for it really is slowly becoming a label for everything and for nothing.'[17] He admits that some formulations in the concluding part of Kasper's review do specify more clearly the direction he was proposing, as when Kasper spoke about how 'a theological interpretation is always then false when it only grounds what is and is not further concrete and critically oriented to action.'[18] All in all, however, there is little conceded in Ratzinger's response to Kasper. So Kasper takes pen in hand again!

On the 'Platonism' to which he considers Ratzinger has now admitted, Kasper points out that it represents such a broad definition of Platonism that it excludes almost nothing, even what is outside the Platonic-philosophical tradition as a whole.[19] But that is not, says Kasper, what he has found in Ratzinger's work: he has found a Platonism that the latter has denied, but has not refuted, in his response to Kasper's review.[20] This Platonism consists in his basing himself on the *visible/invisible* dialectic and then in an espousal of idealism through latently identifying the historically contingent with the necessary, and freedom with necessity. The espousal is *latent*, not *blatant*; but it is not absent, no matter how much Ratzinger wishes it to be.[21]

Ratzinger contented himself with making just two points in the concluding word that he was invited to add to the discussion. First, Kasper had misunderstood him. The definition of Platonism that Kasper suggested was his had *not* been his own but rather a statement of how *Kritischer Katholizismus* construed Platonism by suspiciously placing within it any and every acceptance of abiding truth.[22]

Ratzinger's second point was an attempt to mitigate the so-called squaring of the theological circle, of which he had been accused by Kasper. He did so by pointing out that what he had tried to do was just come a little closer to the perennial question of the *Cur Deus Homo?* under the conditions of our own times but that he had not taken any stance on Rahner's transcendental approach and had not embraced idealism;[23] in other words, he had not made philosophical 'leaps' of the order suggested by Kasper.

On the first point, Ratzinger is undoubtedly correct. Kasper did misunderstand him regarding his definition of Platonism and missed the fact that he was referring to the position of *Kritischer*

Katholizismus on that occasion.[24] On the second point, Ratzinger is not so convincing, having failed to provide an adequate *refutation* of Kasper's charges of latent idealism during the course of their exchange.

All this happened in the 1960s. But the question of Ratzinger's Platonism surfaced again a few years ago when he and Kasper had a dispute about the relationship between the universal Church and particular (or local) Churches. Ratzinger argued for the priority, ontologically and historically, of the universal Church; Kasper accorded a kind of 'equiprimacy' to the universal and to the particular, arguing that, concrete-historically (his typical perspective) you could not have one without the other. Behind the dispute lay the same opposed *philosophical* positions. So, said Kasper, the differences should be allowed to stand, since they did 'not concern church teaching, but theological opinion and various philosophical presuppositions.'[25]

My concern in outlining this Platonism dispute has been, first, to highlight a lasting feature of Ratzinger's theology, present from early on – as Kasper correctly demonstrates – and exercising significant influence on his positions throughout his theological life.[26] Second, with the help of Kasper's critique, I wished to highlight in particular the significance of Ratzinger's Platonist leanings for his unease regarding an emphasis, by theologians, on historical *praxis*, since this unease sets the stage for what was to happen between him and liberation theologies in the 1980s, no matter how much it remained his stated aim to keep his personal theological views in check at that time.

Second Dispute: With Liberation Theologians, Gustavo Gutiérrez especially

In February of 1970, speaking on Vatican radio on the topic 'The Future of the World through the Hope of Men,' Joseph Ratzinger said:

The man of today looks towards the future. His slogan is 'Progress,' not 'Tradition'; 'Hope,' not 'Faith' ... For that to which he looks forward is not, as in the early Church, the kingdom of God, but the kingdom of man, not the return of the Son of Man but the final victory of a rational, free, and brotherly order among men who have discovered themselves.... Thus for the man of today hope no longer means looking for things over which we have no control, but action by our own power. Man expects redemption to come from himself, and he seems to be in a position to provide it. In this way the primacy of the future is linked with the primacy of practice, the primacy of human activity above all other attitudes. Theology, too, is becoming more and more invaded by this attitude. 'Orthopractice' takes the place of orthodoxy, and 'eschatopractice' becomes more important than eschatology.[27]

In these comments, Ratzinger gives voice to a host of concerns that are to dominate his writings in the 1970s and 1980s. Soon to follow will be two important essays – on redemption and salvation respectively – in which he will unfold arguments against various views of salvation that he considers to be anthropologically unsound, above all salvation as 'the makeable future'.[28]

In the 1980s, as head of the Congregation for the Doctrine of the Faith, he will issue two Instructions on liberation theology, *Libertatis Nuntius* (1984) and *Libertatis Conscientia* (1986), as well as a Notification on Leonardo Boff's book *Church, Charism and Power* (1985), with a 'penitential silence' imposed on its author. In 1986, he will publish a critique of Gustavo Gutiérrez's ground-breaking book, *A Theology of Liberation*, and in 1987 he will publish an article on the anthropological vision of the 1986 Instruction.[29]

I shall focus here on what he writes concerning Gutiérrez[30] since this is the sharpest of all his critiques of liberation theology and comes from his theologian's rather than from his Cardinal-Prefect's pen.

Ratzinger sees three levels distinguished in the work of Gutiérrez: (1) liberation of an economic, social and political nature (the *socio-economic* level); (2) liberation for the creation of a new human being in a society of solidarity (the *utopian* level); and (3) liberation from sin (the *theological* level) as making it possible to have communion with God and others.

Ratzinger argues that these three levels collapse effectively into level (2): utopia. Most of what the theological level is interested in, he says, is absorbed by this second level because its concern is making community with others – and that is substantially what has been articulated for level (3). The socio-economic level has no empirically-grounded, well-thought-out conception to present, so the content assigned to it is really sucked up into level (2) also. Thus, in the end, there remains only level (2), the utopian, the level of the *new human being*. Scientific rationality and faith, levels (1) and (3) respectively, insofar as they appear at all, are placed at the service of the utopian level – the driving force of Gutiérrez's whole project.[31]

This means that Gutiérrez views salvation in essentially inner-worldly terms and human beings (thus Marxism) as shouldering the wheel of history in the direction in which it is inexorably already travelling: towards a utopia, an inner-worldly, *material* future (like the 'brotherly order' mentioned on Vatican Radio – indeed, like Karl Marx's classless society). This indicates, Ratzinger says, that Gutiérrez reverses the priority of *logos* over *ethos*. For it is now *ethos* that produces *logos*: from the *matter* of history emerges the *meaningful* future. Ratzinger declares this position to be philosophically irrational: meaning (*Sinn*) cannot come from nonsense (*Unsinn*).

This position, ultimately reliant on the deterministic 'social physics' of French social philosopher, Saint-Simon (1760-1825), embodies a linking of politics and theology *via* metaphysics, and thus necessity, rather than *via* ethics, and thus human freedom.[32] Such a linking is rejected by Joseph Ratzinger, who argues that politics and theology must be linked by the path of ethics.

Following Ratzinger's critiques, Gutiérrez, in his Introduction to the fifteenth anniversary edition of *A Theology of Liberation*, in

1988, says that the preceding years had 'brought serious and relevant critiques that have helped this theological thinking to reach maturity.'[33] They had witnessed an important, if at times painful, debate on liberation theology and had given us magisterial texts 'that advise us about the path to be followed and in various ways spur us on in our quest.'[34] Gutiérrez says of liberation theology's quest that it must maintain a twofold fidelity: to the God of our faith *and* to the Latin American peoples.[35] To aid it in doing so, he offers the following reflections.

First, he concerns himself with the viewpoint of the *poor* – with their irruption into history. The poor are a new presence in history who in the past were always absent. Liberation theology is closely bound up with their presence. These poor have a *social* dimension. Exclusive emphasis on the social and economic aspects of poverty is indeed an exaggeration; yet it remains necessary to call attention to this dimension.[36] What is important is *integral* liberation, which is far greater than liberation from socio-economic deprivation. Thus we are *not* materialists – here Gutiérrez's awareness of Ratzinger's critique is evident, even though he does not mention him explicitly. We require social analysis because this hunts down the *causes* of poverty. The preferential option for the poor is to be maintained – but not to be rendered an *exclusive* option. And the biblical meaning of 'poverty' is to be emphasised.

From the foregoing, Gutiérrez's desire to remain faithful to the God of our faith and to the liberation of the poor peoples of Latin America can already be seen to be operative. He wishes discourse about God and the historical process of liberation not to be separated; hence his distinguishing of three levels of liberation in Christ.[37]

Gutiérrez defends his three levels, but not, as we shall see, without taking into account Ratzinger's critique also. He notes that Puebla (in 1979) made this threefold distinction its own in paragraphs 321-329 of its final document.[38] He points out that each level remains central to his own conception. The first, liberation from situations of *social* oppression, is important but insufficient. Also necessary, he writes, 'is a personal transformation by which we live with profound inner freedom in the face of every kind of servitude, and this is the second dimension or level of liberation.'[39] However, it takes the third level, that of liberation from sin, to attack the deepest root of all servitude: sin, the breaking of friendship with God and with others, ineradicable except by unmerited, redemptive love. These three levels are present and are essential to integral liberation. A collapsing of them all into a single, this-worldly utopia is neither desired nor acceptable:

> There is no slightest tinge of immanentism in this approach to integral liberation. But if any expression I have used may have given the impression that there is, I want to say here as forcefully as I can that any interpretation along those lines is incompatible with my position. Moreover, my repeated emphases (in my writings) on the gratuitousness of God's love as the first and last word in biblical revelation is reliable evidence for this claim.[40]

Michael Sievernich is of the view that Gutiérrez's restatement of his three levels in his 1988 revision amounts to a replacement of utopia with ethics, in line with Joseph Ratzinger's critique.[41]

I might not go so far; but certainly a significant modification, of level (2) above all, is evident. As described above – and I have quoted the actual words of Gutiérrez – there is now, in that 1988 description of the second level, no use of the word *utopia*. Also there is the vigorous denial of immanentism; and it is precisely utopia that Ratzinger condemned as being immanent. So Gutiérrez is really 'conversing' with Ratzinger at this point in a laudable listening tone that Sievernich likens to the greatness of Augustine's self-revisions.[42]

Added to all this is a further word of Gutiérrez, when treating in 1988 of level (2), that of human liberation. He has always emphasised it, he says, in addition to levels (1) and (3), the political and the religious levels, arguing that

emphasis on the mediation of aspects of the human that

are not reducible to the socio-political made it easier to think of all the aspects without confusing them; it also made it possible to speak of God's saving action as all-embracing and unmerited, without reducing it to a purely human set of activities, as well as to interrelate the political and the religious dimensions while also incorporating the needed ethical perspective.[43]

This is certainly a new emphasising of the ethical, if not quite a complete jettisoning of the utopian, as Sievernich has suggested.

Finally, a word from Gutiérrez on *praxis*, again in evident allusion to Ratzinger on that subject. Gutiérrez does not reduce praxis to the practice of social liberations. Rather, he asserts that it is commitment *and* prayer, solidarity with the poor *and* prayer; and that theology reflects critically on *that*.[44] This indeed puts theology in the place of being the 'second step' but not *secondary*.[45] Faith comes first; discourse is second; and each is vital. Faith is the lived faith that finds expression in prayer and commitment. Theology tries, then, to read this lived faith in the light of God's Word. Gutiérrez says:

> There is need of discernment in regard to the concrete forms that Christian commitment takes, and this discernment is accomplished through recourse to the sources of revelation. The ultimate norms of judgment come from the revealed truth that we accept by faith and not from praxis itself.[46]

Thus Ratzinger's accusation that *logos* follows *ethos* in the theology of Gutiérrez seems somewhat exaggerated – or at least wide of the mark.

Ratzinger's exchanges with liberation theology exceed his critique of Gutiérrez and Gutiérrez's responses to that critique. Nonetheless, I have focused on the dispute with Gutiérrez because it comes from Ratzinger's personal theology and indicates how and why this theology is unsympathetic to a liberation approach.

My own view is that Ratzinger does not tease out the nuances of meaning for 'utopia' as Gutiérrez speaks of it, despite the fact that the concept, as it is used in theology, has been noted by others to have many different meanings.[47] Dennis Doyle has pointed out that Gustavo Gutiérrez, in *A Theology of Liberation,* uses the notion of 'utopia' in Karl Mannheim's sense of a thought-form dedicated to working for positive social change.[48] This is a much more theologically acceptable notion of utopia than is attributed to Gutiérrez by Ratzinger.

The account given above of Ratzinger's dispute with Gutiérrez has provided only a flavour of what happened in the 1980s between him and liberation theology. I limited the account to his exchange with Gutiérrez, since that exchange was robust, focused, and carried out, as I said, theologian-to-theologian.

Overall, I consider that Ratzinger's critiques – and I include here documents of his Congregation – gave space to people who have no concern for changing the mechanisms that cause poverty and and keep the poor in poverty, to assume that they had an easy ally in the Church authorities, in spite of how the Instructions of 1984 and 1986 attempted to support the aspiration of the poor to liberation. Also, due to deficiencies in how the dialogue with liberation theologians was undertaken, the critiques proved overly subduing, even stifling. Views on this differ, of course, but I recall that it was an era in which many theologians were very discouraged.

6

QUAESTIONES DISPUTATAE: THEOLOGICAL DISSENT

During the twenty-three years that Joseph Ratzinger headed the Congregation for the Doctrine of the Faith (CDF), he penned many theological texts of his own and also numerous ecclesiastical documents. Did his personal theological views exercise an influence on the positions taken by his Congregation? They did.

Even a brief glance at Ratzinger's texts from the 1960s and 1970s reveals already an approach to theology that was to put him decidedly at odds with the liberation theology about which he was to write *Instructions* in the 1980s as Prefect of the CDF. One need only cast one's mind back to his disagreements with Kasper and Gutierrez (explored in the previous chapter) to recall how he differed with these two on the starting-point of theology and on the role envisaged for *praxis* in it.

But his lack of enthusiasm for according a significant role to praxis in theology was evident already in much earlier works, for example, in a text from 1975, in which he voiced scepticism about what he derisively termed 'almighty praxis', as well as in a 1970 Vatican Radio talk in which he noted that 'orthopractice' had taken the place of orthodoxy.[1] So what he had to say, as CDF Prefect, about liberation theology during the 1980s could hardly have been expected to be welcoming of that theology, given his own theological preferences. Indeed, to have anticipated otherwise would have been unrealistic, since no amount of epistemological gymnastics could have kept the judgments of Ratzinger the theologian and Ratzinger the Prefect in entirely separate compartments.[2]

The matter of Ratzinger's personal theological preferences became a concern for theologians in the 1980s, following the publication of *The Ratzinger Report*, his gloomy book-length interview with Italian journalist, Vittorio Messori.[3] As David Gibson said in his recent book, its appearance 'was a bombshell ... Ratzinger's blunt observations and criticisms created headlines and cemented his hardline reputation.'[4]

At a press conference in Rome on May 30, 1985, Ratzinger stated that his views in *The Ratzinger Report* were 'completely personal' and did not in any way 'implicate the institutions of the Holy See.'[5] Richard McCormick, reflecting on that remark a few years later, said that it raised theological worries of the first magnitude.[6]

Nor was McCormick the only theologian who was alarmed by what Ratzinger was saying during the 1980s. In an issue of the English Dominican journal, *New Blackfriars*, in June 1985, several British theologians voiced concerns about *The Ratzinger Report*. Nicholas Lash stated that he could not 'share the Cardinal's pessimism,' a pessimism that he traced, at least partly, to his 'classicist' perspective (recall Bernard Lonergan), an interpretative framework that 'also helps to explain why he should seek to make his erstwhile colleagues, the theologians, particular scapegoats for our plight.'[7] Eamon Duffy spoke of 'the lurid and simplistic world of easy dualisms from which Cardinal Ratzinger's oracular voice seems to emanate' and, following on from this more general observation, questioned Ratzinger's 'idealized account of the Church' (in the polarity church/world) as well as his assertion – above all, and with a straight face, as head of the CDF – that the Church had taken on the '"best values that two centuries of liberal culture had produced".'[8]

Thus it is not unreasonable to say that theologians were discouraged by the pessimistic views that were emerging from Ratzinger in the 1980s, particularly as these views appeared to envisage a more constricting relationship of the magisterium to theologians, above all in the area of moral theology.[9]

For this reason – rather than examining disputes between particular theologians (of whom there were many) and the CDF in the 1980s (and 1990s) – I wish to probe here what lay behind Ratzinger's dealings with theologians, at the time, who dissented from certain non-infallible teachings of the magisterium.[10] So what I am really probing in this chapter is Ratzinger's own views on theological *dissent.*

The Magisterium and Theologians

The relevant texts for Ratzinger's views on dissent are, first, *The Ratzinger Report;*[11] second, a 1986 talk in Toronto on 'The Church as an Essential Dimension of Theology';[12] and third, the CDF *Instruction,* in 1990, on 'The Ecclesial Vocation of the Theologian.'[13]

There is a fourth text also; and it came about like this. The 1990 *Instruction* drew a robust response from the theological community – in Germany and Austria, in Latin America, in the United States, and elsewhere – that caused Ratzinger to re-issue the text that he had read at the press conference introducing the *Instruction* as well as to publish some further remarks in response to the 'polemic' (his own word) that followed the *Instruction's* appearance. The press conference text and those 'further remarks' are what I have in mind here as the fourth text.[14] I shall not have space to treat each text fully here, but I shall draw on all in the course of my reflections below.

Ratzinger and Dissent: An Attitude of Suspicion

Cardinal Ratzinger, in the 1980s, had a strong tendency to view Catholics – and especially theologians – who dissented from non-infallible teachings of the Church as *misconceiving* the nature of the Church and its teaching office in some way; and he pointed to such misconception more than once.[15] In *The Ratzinger Report,* he stated:

> In a world in which, at bottom, many believers are gripped by scepticism, the conviction of the Church that there is *one truth,* and that this one truth can as such be

recognized, expressed and also clearly defined within certain bounds, appears scandalous. It is also experienced as offensive by many Catholics who have lost sight of the essence of the Church. The Church is, however, not only a human organization; she also has a deposit to defend that does not belong to her, the proclamation and transmission of which is guaranteed through a teaching office that brings it close to men of all times in a fitting manner.[16]

The mentality of many theologians, however, was not, as Ratzinger saw it, to view the Church's teaching office as has just been described. Rather certain theologians *relativised* what the teaching office had to say as but an expression of 'the archaic Roman theology' rather than an expression of the faith of the Church (of which their own theological hypotheses were held to articulate the authentic meaning).[17]

This was a misconception of the Church and of the magisterium, Ratzinger said, and it even led to a kind of parallel magisterium of theologians.[18] It not uncommonly conceived the Church's teaching authority as authoritarian and anti-democratic, whereas in fact (thus Ratzinger) it was the magisterium that had 'something like a democratic character: it defends the common faith, which recognizes no distinction of rank between the learned and the simple.'[19] But not all saw the magisterium thus – and therein was expressed their misconception of the Church and its teaching office that Ratzinger considered to be one of the roots of the crisis of the time.[20]

The Ratzinger Report was so negative about any form of theological dissent from any kind of Church teaching[21] that theologians came to wonder what space, if any, remained for them to pursue any sort of critical work. Ratzinger held the view that, in moral theology, which he saw as 'the main locus of the tensions between Magisterium and theologians,'[22] the alternatives had become: oppose modern society or oppose the magisterium; and the latter approach was growing – above all in the opulent West. He began to talk of dissent, certainly in regard to sexual morality, as a bourgeois, mainly North American, middle-class thing; people who were benefiting from life in an affluent society were seeking to make compromises with it.[23] This was the case with regard to contraception, pre-marital sex, masturbation and homosexuality.[24]

As for liberation theology, many of its ideas had been distilled by theologians of European origin in 'laboratories' of thought foreign to the Latin American poor, although it was these very poor that liberation theology purported to opt for.[25] The reality was that it was the poor, the uneducated simple believers – the 'little ones' in Latin America *and* in the opulent societies of North America and Europe – who were 'least protected from distortions' and whom, therefore, the magisterium saw itself duty-bound to protect.[26] He knew the threat their faith was under, from reports that landed on his desk and through letters that he received from what he believed to be 'typical Catholics.'[27]

One cannot help but raise questions here. Does the CDF in fact receive representative mail? Is extolling the simple faithful not a justification for ignoring the un-simple faithful: educated men and women who are also members of the Church but who wish to contribute reflection based on their genuine competencies – theology included? If they are educated and prosperous, must they necessarily also be compromisers with the *Zeitgeist?* Ratzinger's rhetoric was going too far here, as indeed was his suspicion of theologians. He said:

> I wonder at the adroitness of theologians who manage to represent the exact opposite of what it written in clear documents of the Magisterium in order afterward to set forth this inversion with skilled dialectical devices as the 'true' meaning of the documents in question.[28]

Asking the Impossible of Theologians

In the atmosphere just described, a tense relationship between the Prefect of the CDF and theologians became inevitable. Most alarming was the fact that dissent of any kind – even very careful, responsible disagreement with non-infallible teachings – seemed increasingly to be outlawed, even as a possibility, since it was seen as coming from erroneous conceptions of the Church and relativistic approaches to its teachings.

Behind Cardinal Ratzinger's judgments that theologians were misconceiving the Church lay certain ecclesiological assumptions that hearkened back to a mentality reminiscent of Pius XII at the time of *Humani Generis* (1950), when a highly juridical understanding of Church teaching obtained and all dissent was effectively proscribed once the Pope – in his exercise of the ordinary magisterium – had spoken on a matter. It was the era of *Roma locuta est, causa finita est.*[29]

This conception of the ordinary papal magisterium may have been understandable in the context in which it flourished; but it was, nonetheless, a relatively new development (nineteenth century) that treated teaching in a highly *juridical* way.[30] When ecclesiologist Francis Sullivan was commenting, in 1991, on the 'one-sidedly juridical approach to the question of the collaboration between theologians and the magisterium' that he found in the CDF *Instruction on the Ecclesial Vocation of the Theologian* (n. 22), he said of such an approach:

> The danger in the juridical approach of this Instruction is that it suggests that ultimately there is only one kind of teaching authority in the Church, the hierarchical, and that all teaching authority must necessarily be a participation in this.[31]

Am I asserting here that Ratzinger's juridical emphasis in the *Instruction* was a return to the mentality of Pius XII at the time of *Humani Generis* and that it outlawed, in principle, all dissent by theologians, even from the ordinary magisterium? No, I am not asserting exactly that; but I am asserting (with Sullivan – and he with Avery Dulles) that the *Instruction*, in its return to a certain juridicism, tended to give that impression.[32]

That it did not actually rule out the possibility of all disagreement with official teaching is clear, on careful reading, because both in the *Instruction* itself and in Ratzinger's own 'further remarks' on it, he did not proscribe all disagreement with the magisterium – in the latter he even spoke of 'cases of loyal dissent' (an inexact rendering of *Fragen eines loyalen Dissenses*)[33] – although he did find unacceptable, indeed incomprehensible, any recourse to the mass media on the part of theologians who dissented.

It was clear that he envisaged use of the mass media in negative terms, seeing it essentially as mobilising the media *against* the magisterium; and thus he viewed *public* dissent as being always unacceptable.[34] In the CDF *Instruction* itself, the word 'dissent' was reserved to 'public opposition to the Magisterium of the Church'[35] and so, since *that* was prohibited, one could say that the *Instruction* simply outlawed dissent.

However, since other forms of disagreement with the magisterium were not excluded by it, this statement would be misleading. Francis Sullivan's conclusion is thus entirely correct: 'it should be clear how misleading it would be to say that the CDF has ruled out all dissent by theologians in the Catholic Church, without explaining what this Instruction means by "dissent".'[36] It means *public* opposing of the magisterium; and it prohibits it.

Here, however, two crucial points must be raised. The first is whether it is *possible* for a theologian to disagree with the magisterium in a manner that avoids all public disclosure of the disagreement. Opinions vary here. Richard McCormick has thought, for some time now, that it is impossible. In this age of communications, the reporters are at the door. In any case, theology is a public enterprise, seeking (recall Lonergan) to mediate between a culture and a religion.[37]

I would add: was it not a bit disingenuous of Cardinal Ratzinger to suggest that the public dimension could be avoided – and surprising, given the fact that he himself had been no stranger to press conferences and had published, already at that time, one book-length interview with a journalist on topics concerning Church and theology (to be followed, indeed, by two even longer interviews with journalist Peter Seewald in 1996 and 2002 respectively)? That is more material than all the theologians his Congregation investigated – combined – had given to journalists on tensions in the Church! [38]

Charles Curran has stated that, particularly in relation to the public action taken by the CDF in relation to him, it was ultimately for the good of the Church that he made matters public and that he had tried to do so with care, using the occasions as a teaching moment.[39] Francis Sullivan showed that Ratzinger took for granted that a theologian's disagreement with the magisterium would be communicated to theological colleagues, for example in scholarly journals and at theological conferences. Sullivan then added that, once this happened, it would acquire a public aspect (thus becoming 'dissent' as the *Instruction* defines this), since material shared at conferences and even in scholarly journals 'will inevitably get into the popular media.' Sullivan went on to state:

> I think that one could rightly invoke the principle of the double effect. For sufficient reason, one can permit an undesirable effect which one can foresee but does not intend. I believe that the sufficient reason here is the necessity of communication among theologians precisely so that they can expose their ideas to the criticism of their colleagues.[40]

One can scarcely improve on these remarks of Sullivan. They make clear that what Ratzinger asked for in the *Instruction* was unrealistic – and impossible to achieve in a concrete situation of disagreement with the ordinary magisterium by a theologian.

I mentioned *two* crucial points above. The second is as follows. While it is the case that Ratzinger, as theologian and as Prefect, did not exclude absolutely every form of disagreement with the magisterium, he did provide evidence – particularly in his 1986 Toronto talk – of his personal attitude concerning theological disagreement with non-infallible Church teachings.

The 'heroes' of his Toronto talk were Karl Barth, Erik Peterson, Heinrich Schlier and Romano Guardini. They had all come to grasp, each in his own way, the intrinsic connection between Church and theology. Their historical circumstances occasioned their doing so: the collapse of the classical-liberal theological approach between the wars (Barth, Peterson) and the fate of the Church at the hands of National Socialism (Schlier, Guardini).[41] To the latter pair Ratzinger's name could almost be added, because the horrors of Nazism furnished him with an abiding trust in the Church as the guarantor of truth and freedom.

Now, having placed himself in such company as he contemplated the ecclesial identity of theology – two of the figures had even found their way from the Evangelical to the Catholic Church (Peterson, Schlier) – Ratzinger was already expressing his disinclination towards finding any positive value in *questioning* the teaching of the Church and his inclination to emphasise conversion, receiving, humbly submitting, as closest to the heart of the theologian's undertaking.[42]

A letter from Ratzinger to *The Tablet* in 1991 illustrates his personal attitude to dissent. In 1972, he had made a suggestion, as a theologian, that included norms that could be implemented in pastoral practice permitting divorced and remarried Catholics to receive the sacraments. However, Pope John Paul II, in 1984, in *Familiaris Consortio* (n. 84), spoke against such reception; and Ratzinger made it clear that, to such a judgment of the magisterium he would – and in fact did – submit.[43] Nor did he change his view as Benedict XVI when the matter came up in the first Synod of Bishops of his pontificate in 2005, even though earlier in that year he had responded to a question from an Italian priest to the effect that the matter deserved further study. *Roma locuta est, causa finita est* remained the case for Joseph Ratzinger, even when he had become Benedict XVI.

Reformable Procedures?

The kind of interaction that occurs between theologians under investigation and the CDF, which is investigating them, raises questions today, particularly in an age that is conscious of human rights and transparency of procedures. Even Cardinal Ratzinger, when he was Prefect of the CDF, showed himself to be aware 'that the right of the individual theologian must be protected,'[44] although he made this point in a context in which he was emphasising the right of the community to have the 'common good' of ecclesial faith protected. In the 1990 *Instruction,* he showed himself to be aware that the procedures that are followed by the magisterium in arriving at a judgment about a theologian's intellectual positions could be improved, but he argued that this did not mean that they were unjust and in violation of the theologian's rights:

> The judgment expressed by the Magisterium in such circumstances is the result of a thorough investigation conducted according to established procedures which afford the interested party the opportunity to clear up possible misunderstandings of his thought. This judgment, however, does not concern the person of the theologian but the intellectual positions which he has publicly espoused. *The fact that these procedures can be improved does not mean that they are contrary to justice and right.* To speak in this instance of a violation of human rights is out of place for it indicates a failure to recognize the proper hierarchy of these rights as well as the nature of the ecclesial community and her common good. Moreover, the theologian who is not disposed to think with the Church ('sentire cum Ecclesia') contradicts the commitment he freely and knowingly accepted to teach in the name of the Church.[45]

Two questions arise here. The first relates to the procedures: if they 'can be improved', then what is it about them that admits of improvement? It must be some lack, for if there is no lack there is no 'improvability'; there is nothing that can be reformed in the direction of greater fairness, or justice, or thoroughness, or some such good quality. If, indeed, there is a lack, then improvement becomes a duty; for we are talking about the Church and its treatment of its members here. The *Instruction* is silent about what could actually be improved; nor have I witnessed Ratzinger be more specific elsewhere.

Many theologians (Schillebeeckx, Boff, Curran – to name but a few) have indicated, from their experience of the CDF's procedures, certain definite limitations.[46] These should therefore be the subject of regular scrutiny (*ecclesia semper reformanda*) because complete justice is ever the goal, but never the achievement, of any temporal reality, including an ecclesial temporal reality such as the CDF.[47]

The second question that arises from the words of the *Instruction* quoted above has to do with the words 'the theologian who is not disposed to think with the Church.' It seems to me that there is an assumption in those words that, when a theologian writes something that the CDF considers it necessary to investigate, the theologian is already seen as someone who is not disposed to think with the Church.

I find this assumption odd. No theologian – recall Boff in 1985: 'I prefer to walk with the Church than alone with my theology' – *wants* to find him or herself *not* thinking with the Church. That is painful and isolating; thus it is difficult to imagine it being willed. It does happen, of course, that a theologian will sometimes have difficulties with a teaching. And if he or she deals with these along the lines that are indicated in the *Instruction on the Ecclesial Vocation of the Theologian* (under the heading 'Collaborative Relations'),[48] then the words 'not disposed to think with the Church' are not applicable. However, if it is a matter of public opposition to the magisterium (although this is scarcely avoidable nowadays, as we have seen), then the theologian is engaged in what Cardinal Ratzinger really means by 'dissent' and the words 'not disposed to think with the Church' clearly are applicable, as their appearance in the section entitled 'The Problem of Dissent' indicates. I do not think that such application is warranted – certainly it is not in every case of public disagreement with the magisterium. Motives are being attributed here.

Is Dialogue Possible?

Important in all of the above is to consider how, in the matter of dissent, theological dialogue-partners were looked at. Were they in fact envisaged as *dialogue*-partners at all by the CDF? In much of Ratzinger's theological writing, his underlying concern is *humanity*. Thus, even today – long after the dispute over liberation theology – he still, when writing about initiatives to improve *material* well-being, emphasises the soul, the whole person, integral liberation.[49] But in dealing with dissenting theologians, with bishops, with lay Catholics, the emphasis seems to me to have been too much on the human being as *receiver* and insufficiently on the person as a thinker, a contributor, an expert in some relevant area who is willing and able to share his or her competence.

If authority, rather than understanding, is the theologian's final resting place with regard to a teaching, then can he or she be really said to be truly commending the teaching; or is she/he simply holding it, and recommending that it be held, at a less mature level of moral development reflective of 'Kohlberg's preconventional level of reasoning (obey or be punished)'?[50] A theologian who is simply an echo, but never a critical questioner, of ordinary magisterial teaching, exhibits a truncated, an immature, humanity. Likewise a bishop who never says anything controversial, 'for fear of getting into trouble with Rome.' But *somehow*, in the Ratzinger-John Paul II era, such theologians and bishops were the ideal; and that contradicts the very fullness of humanity – and our striving for it – that Ratzinger himself actually espouses.

That has been more serious, in the realm of all the *quaestiones disputatae*, than the actual disputes themselves. For we are meant to believe with all our hearts, all our souls – and all our *minds*.

7

RESISTING THE 'DICTATOR-SHIP OF RELAVITISM'

At the time of his election as Pope, Cardinal Ratzinger was already well known as an opponent of relativism. In his homily before the conclave that elected him Pope, he used a phrase – 'dictatorship of relativism' – that quickly became famous. He said:

> Today, having a clear faith based on the Creed of the Church is often labeled as fundamentalism. Whereas relativism, that is, letting oneself be 'tossed here and there, carried about by every wind of doctrine', seems the only attitude that can cope with modern times. We are building a dictatorship of relativism that does not recognize anything as definitive and whose ultimate goal consists only of one's own ego and desires.[1]

His key concern in these words was the recognising of nothing as definitive. It comes up repeatedly in his discussions of relativism, and it troubles him deeply. About a year and a half after his election as Pope, while addressing the bishops of Ontario on their *ad limina* visit, he told them that, above all in their schools, Catholic influence was needed in order to overcome the 'particularly insidious obstacle' posed by 'that relativism which, recognizing nothing as definitive, leaves as the ultimate criterion only the self with its desires.'[2] Where does this recognising of nothing as definitive come from that leaves the self prey to just itself; and what are its implications for Christian faith?

The Roots and the Consequences of Relativism

Ratzinger, speaking in 1996 to German journalist Peter Seewald concerning the contemporary 'current' of relativism, suggested that it grew out of various roots and that it posed far-reaching consequences for Christianity:

> For one thing, it seems to modern man undemocratic, intolerant, and also incompatible with the scientist's necessary scepticism to say that we have the truth and that something else is not the truth, or is only fragmentary truth. Precisely this democratic understanding of life and the concomitant idea of toleration has made the question of whether we are entitled to go on with our Christian self-understanding a burning one.[3]

So, relativism emerges as the accompaniment of a wish to appear democratic, tolerant, humble about one's grasp of truth; it springs from the climate of our times. Democracy defends the right of each person to his or her own viewpoint, so much so, indeed, that it seems to imply a tolerance that asks us to relativise our own positions and to shrink from putting them forward as *true*.

This is rather odd, as Ratzinger indicates elsewhere when he points out that democracy itself requires a non-relativistic kernel in order to function. It is constructed, ultimately, around human rights that are inviolable, and their inviolability is not 'up for grabs' but recognised as definitive.[4] It is also odd, I would add, because the very right for which democracy fights – namely, that one *may* freely assert a given position – is diminished by the *sotto voce* idea that one may *not* do so too strongly, as this would be perceived as being intolerant towards others' positions. In all of this, the casualty is *truth*, not only the idea that nothing may be asserted as true but, eventually, even the idea that truth can be known at all.

Where does this leave Christian faith, which has always been linked to truth? Muzzled. Not permitted to be itself. Dictated to by the requirements of the relativist creed. Ratzinger asserts himself vigorously against this 'dictatorship.'

He points out that Christian faith involves a claim to truth – a truth that has been *received*, given to us, *not made* by ourselves,[5] and that we cannot abandon this claim (or the responsibilities that come with receiving it) in a manner that 'leaves us simply blundering about among various types of tradition.'[6] Were we to do so, we would be succumbing to a relativism of religious traditions, saying, in effect, that Christianity belonged among the panoply of the religions in general – true, in its own way, as they are, in their own ways, but no more. To say this would be to abandon what I pointed to in an earlier chapter as the first 'facial feature' of Ratzinger's theology: namely, that the God of philosophy and the God of faith are *one*.[7] This 'facial feature' constitutes a principle that expresses the radical monotheism of the Bible and ensures, thereby, that Christianity's claim to *truth* stands and that the Christian faith tradition cannot simply be relegated to the status of 'one tradition among many.'[8]

Ratzinger's fight against the contemporary relativistic mentality can be seen, in the light of this key principle, to be imperative. Were he to ignore the relativistic challenge, he would simply be allowing Christianity to be demolished at its very centre.

Furthermore, this would be showing contempt for God. For if we go to the extreme of 'dropping all claims to truth,'[9] denying that God can *gift* us with the truth about himself, then is not this putting limits on what God can and cannot do? Ratzinger inquires: 'Is it not contempt for God to say that we have been born blind and that truth is not our issue?'[10]

Many assert that it is arrogant to say that God can *give* us the truth. Ratzinger argues that, in the end, it is the relativist who is arrogant, because it is arrogant to *deny* that God can give us the truth. We must be humble: we do not possess truth, but we are able to *receive* it. Indeed Ratzinger once pointed out, drawing on Romano Guardini, that humility consists here not in retreating from naming God and being voiceless before the ineffable (as is so fashionable today), but rather in bowing before the scandal that God can and does *do* the unimaginable: become human, now true God *and* true man, in the historical Jesus of Nazareth.[11]

Also, saying that we have received the truth in this way does not equate to an arrogance that is unable to recognise how faith affirms 'that the unlikeness between what is known by us and reality itself is infinitely greater than the likeness.'[12] In the background here is the notion of analogy, of which Joseph Ratzinger is a repeated proponent. He sees *analogy* as keeping us ever mindful of the human being's limitations with regard to truth, but he points out that, within the human boundaries that do obtain, analogy (which 'can always be broadened and deepened') does declare truth and is not to be equated with 'metaphor'.[13] Thus, while Ratzinger rejects relativ*ism*, he has no difficulty saying that our statements about God admit of a certain *relativising*. The words of Saint Augustine are never far from his thoughts; and it was Augustine who remarked that, if we have understood, then it is not God.

Relativism in Theology: Some Key Texts

Ratzinger has written a great deal concerning relativism, certainly since the early 1990s.[14] Only a few texts can be alluded to here, two of which, in particular, are really of special importance. The first is an address, in 1996, at Guadalajara in Mexico, to the presidents of the Doctrinal Commissions of the Bishops' Conferences of Latin America;[15] the second is the Declaration *Dominus Jesus*, which emerged in the year 2000 from the Congregation for the Doctrine of the Faith when Ratzinger was its Prefect.[16] These texts may be taken together, even though the latter is a document of the CDF, because many of the same concerns are expressed in each and, in the case of the second, Ratzinger's authorship is, in my view, hardly in dispute (even if others collaborated with him).

Relativism in theology was the central concern of both documents. *Dominus Jesus* referred to 'certain presuppositions' on the basis of which theological proposals were being developed that led 'Christian revelation and the mystery of Jesus Christ and the Church [to] lose their character of absolute truth and salvific universality', or at least to have these cast under shadows of doubt and uncertainty. Among these 'certain presuppositions', the text named 'relativistic attitudes toward truth itself, according to which what is true for some would not be true for others.'[17] It was a central task of *Dominus Jesus* to provide a remedy for this relativism. The document said:

> As a remedy for this relativistic mentality, which is be-coming ever more common, it is necessary above all to reassert the definitive and complete character of the revelation of Jesus Christ.[18]

The point was: there are Christian truths, definitive in nature, that are being cast aside due to the march of relativism. And these need to be firmly recalled for Catholics, so that theology will meet the challenges of consistency with the contents of the faith and responsiveness to the culture's needs.[19]

Catholics, then, were the addressees of *Dominus Jesus*. And although it was a text that dealt much with interreligious dialogue and ecumenism, it was not intended as a document of dialogue, but rather as a kind of 'in-house' document for Catholics ('Bishops, theologians, and all the Catholic faithful', n. 3) recalling for them 'certain indispensable elements of Christian doctrine, which may help theological reflection in developing solutions consistent with the contents of the faith and responsive to the pressing needs of contemporary culture' (n. 3).

The document begins with the accent on *mission*, the Church's mission to proclaim salvation in Christ to all. It *then* points out that the Church's use of the practice of *dialogue* today does not replace mission but rather accompanies it, as 'all men and women who are saved share, though differently, in the same mystery of salvation in Jesus Christ through his Spirit' (n. 2).[20] *Dominus Jesus* also ends with the accent on the Church's evangelizing mission, pointing out that interreligious dialogue is but one part of that mission *ad gentes* of the Church (n. 22).

Moving on with this emphasis on mission, the Declaration states that 'the Church's constant missionary proclamation is endangered today by relativistic theories which seek to justify religious pluralism, not only *de facto* but also *de iure (or in principle)'* (n. 4). Indeed what occasioned the Declaration was the pervading of Western Christian consciousness by the idea, today, that all the religions are, for their followers, *equally* valid ways of salvation.[21] An idea such as this, which constitutes just such a *de iure* justification of religious pluralism as Ratzinger was seen to refer to above, can be traced to writers such as (but certainly not only) John Hick. He is not mentioned in *Dominus Jesus* (which confines itself to councils, popes and Church Fathers). But Ratzinger refers to him in his Guadalajara address: he believes that Hicks's relativist viewpoint sees the Church's faith in Jesus as fundamentalist, insisting, in its stead, that true dialogue cannot take place unless the faith-convictions of all religions participating in the dialogue are placed on the same, equal level. Ratzinger has already clarified what he understands by this approach to dialogue in his Guadalajara address:

> [D]ialogue in the relativist sense means setting one's own position or belief on the same level with what the other person believes, ascribing to it, on principle, no more of the truth than to the position of the other person. Only if my fundamental presupposition is that the other person may be just as much in the right as I am, or even more so, can any dialogue take place at all.[22]

Ratzinger finds this to represent 'a different meaning' for the notion of 'dialogue' from 'the concept of dialogue which certainly held an important place in the Platonic and in the Christian tradition.'[23] And, as he indicated later in remarks while presenting *Dominus Jesus* to the public, he finds it to be a travesty, too, of the concept of 'dialogue' found and rooted in the Second Vatican Council, which never separated dialogue from proclamation and never did away with the truth in the name of practising dialogue.[24] Ratzinger makes clear, in a text on Jewish-Christian relations, that he does not think abandoning the quest for truth enriches the process of interreligious dialogue:

The religions can encounter one another only by delving more deeply into the truth, not by giving it up. Scepticism does not unite. Nor does sheer pragmatism.[25]

And again, in the same text:

The answer, I think, is that mission and dialogue must no longer be antitheses, but must penetrate each other. Dialogue is not random conversation, but aims at persuasion, at discovering the truth. Otherwise it is worthless.[26]

The concerns of the Guadalajara address and of *Dominus Jesus* were both theological and anthropological. God is not so shrouded in mystery that all knowledge of God must remain fragmentary and vague, with nothing positive at all being able to be said about God; for God has come close, become visible and approachable, in his Son Jesus.[27] And the human being is not so incapable of truth that it is his/her lot to stumble around in complete uncertainty; for we are created for truth and, though we have sinned and become beings of untruth, our orientation to truth is still there (however impaired) – and truth has stolen close to us redemptively in the loving self-disclosure of God to us in Jesus Christ.[28]

However, belief in all of these things is becoming impossible in the current of metaphysical and religious relativism that is gradually proposing itself to the world at large as the only truly democratic, tolerant philosophical stance and the only acceptable attitude in a mutli-religious world in which the religions must dialogue and cooperate.[29] The problem with this is that it means that

The relativist elimination of Christology, and most certainly of ecclesiology, now becomes a central commandment of religion.[30]

But it was against christological and ecclesiological relativism that Prefect Ratzinger published *Dominus Jesus* (and his Guadalajara address). Interreligious dialogue is not served by such a renunciation of truth, even if, at first glance, this might seem to be 'a necessary condition of the capacity for peace.'[31]

How, then, Is Dialogue To Be Envisaged?

At the end of *Dominus Jesus* Ratzinger makes it clear that the *equality* he sees as being a presupposition of interreligious dialogue refers to the parties who are involved in the dialogue. It does not refer to doctrinal content; and it certainly does not refer to Jesus Christ, who is God made man, in relation to the founders of the other religions.[32] Thus dialogue, for him, belongs above all to the evangelizing mission of the Church and, as such, is much less about hearing from, appreciating and being enriched by the other than it is simply about proclamation – proclamation of the truth revealed by God in Christ and entrusted to the Church as its mission. It seems to me – and we shall explore this just a little in what follows – that Jesus himself did not dialogue in quite such a one-sided way. The Australian theologian Gerard Hall has suggested that

> religious dialogue as perceived in the document is so subordinate to proclamation, and so marginally conceived with respect to the Church's mission of evangelisation, it loses most of its integrity as an act of Christian witness.[33]

Hall goes on to say that dialogue then 'runs the danger of being 'manipulated' into a means of proclamation' and that this is a position not advocated by Pope John Paul II's encyclical letter *Redemptoris Missio* (1990) and other documents.[34] Hall is aware that *Redemptoris Missio* gives priority to proclamation over dialogue, but argues that it (and other magisterial documents) exhibit 'an at least cautious optimism' with regard to the role of dialogue that is absent in *Dominus Jesus*, because the latter, viewing the world in which dialogue is to occur as rife with the 'relativistic mentality', falls consequently into a 'negative – at times even aggressive – tone.'[35]

Theologians might be expected to argue with such a tone; the interesting thing about *Dominus Jesus* is that, following its publication, a number of Ratzinger's fellow cardinals and bishops – archbishops, indeed – spoke of the tone, language and lack of ecumenical sensitivity of the document in a manner considerably more severe than anything I have referred to here.[36]

In his vigorous opposing of relativism and his heightened concern to enunciate the principles and highlight the fixed points that bind Roman Catholics in interreligious dialogue, Ratzinger has espoused a kind of strategy of 'getting things clear' beforehand and *then* of according dialogue its place. This strategy has the effect of conferring surety on Catholics while 'at home', as it were, but uncertainty once they venture forth, for in venturing forth their primary commitment must be to the proclaiming of Christian truth (see *Dominus Jesus*, 22).

That Ratzinger would place the emphasis on Catholics holding true to their christological and ecclesiological heritage – above all in the face of possible temptations to relativise these – I find un-derstandable. However to do so in the manner adopted in *Dominus Jesus* was found by many, inside and outside the Church, to be rather 'hard-line'. Now that Cardinal Ratzinger has become Pope, and is speaking in a softer, more pastoral voice, people can tend to forget that he is more than capable of turning up the heat under others and, in fairness, of taking the heat himself. Indeed the September 2006 controversy in Regensburg is an example of this.

In Regensburg, Benedict/Ratzinger did what Ratzinger char-acteristically does. Instead of bowing to political correctness as the 'dictatorship of relativism' demands, he followed, as he did in *Dominus Jesus*, his preferred method of 'getting things clear before-hand' and then taking the fallout. In Regensburg what he got clear was that there could be no marrying of religion and violence: that to spread faith by force was to act contrary to reason and hence to act contrary to God's own nature, because God is *logos*, reason, word.[37] God could not command what was intrinsically unreason-able without violating God's own nature.

In making this point, Benedict referred to a dialogue, from the late fourteenth century, between an erudite Byzantine emperor sympathetic to his own understanding of God as intrinsically rational and an educated Persian for whom the utter transcendence of God – even beyond the category of rationality – would have been decisively important.[38] Benedict then cited, not as his own opinion, a remark of the emperor about Mohammed commanding the spreading of faith by the sword, the purpose of this citation not being to condemn Mohammed but solely to highlight that a failure to act according to reason (by violent converting, for example) is contrary to the nature of God.[39] But 'fine-line' distinctions proved insufficiently consoling outside the university context, and the result of Benedict's remarks was a furore not dissimilar to what he had experienced after the publication of *Dominus Jesus*, but this time with the Muslim community (as was to be expected) at the forefront. Christian acts of violence, of which history was said to be replete, would have served Benedict just as well, many newspaper articles opined.

Some people have argued that Benedict was very surprised by what happened after Regensburg, thinking his remark there nothing more than an academic historical reference useful for the illustration of an important point. Others – and I among them – believe that Benedict XVI, while not intending to offend, knew what he was doing in the sense that he was making a vital point about dialogue between the religions: this dialogue must welcome rational critique – certainly the kind of critique that questions irrational or voluntaristic approaches of the sort referred to in that Regensburg address. Questions of truth (*is* God rational?) must not be sacrificed to the (relativistic) demands of 'political correctness'. Benedict's view of interreligious dialogue is that it will be robust: it will not sacrifice the quest for truth and the use of sharp reason, but will maintain them. Yet the signs are present that he is also continuing to reflect on how interreligious dialogue can proceed in a more eirenic and fraternal way.

Recently, in the wake of the Regensburg controversy, while speaking to some German bishops on their *ad limina* visit to Rome,

Benedict XVI underscored with them the importance of dialogue *and*, in the dialogue, of *knowing* Islam as well as, of course, their Catholicism. Benedict then went on to speak to the German Bishops about Jesus Christ being their point of reference in the dialogue.[40]

What did this mean? Unheeding proclamation? I have been thinking about this. How could it be understood in a way that allows the dialogue to take place really well, as Jesus' dialogues did, for example, with Nicodemus, or the woman at the well, the man born blind, or Martha (in chapters 3, 4, 9 and 11 respectively of the Fourth Gospel)?

The American theologian, John F. Haught, once spoke movingly of how Christ can be a, nay *the*, point of reference in interreligious dialogue, such that this dialogue can truly be a giving of space, a moving over, a *kenosis* in which we let go and let be – let the other *be* other – and, in this way, come better to understand both our selves and them.[41]

I discovered similar (and surprising) remarks on the part of Ratzinger around the time that *Dominus Jesus* was published. In speaking of Incarnation, he points to its at once apophatic and tangible character: here God becomes so concrete in history that he can be laid hold of, yet simultaneously, in his kenosis, he is truly hidden and mysterious.[42] Here there is true paradox: a vulnerability, a defencelessness, that cannot overpower and, at the selfsame moment, a real and concrete truth that can neither be resisted nor fully fathomed. This paradox prompts Ratzinger to the reflection: 'God's kenosis is itself the place where the religions can come into contact without arrogant claims to domination.'[43] In this, surely, we find an 'opening' that is softer in tone than *Dominus Jesus* and that promises a less 'hard-line' approach to interreligious conversation than that document adopted.

I can think of one other opening that would temper the tone of *Dominus Jesus*. This has to do with the relationship between Jesus Christ, the kingdom of God and the Church. *Dominus Jesus* seeks to counter one-sided accentuations such as are found in approaches that call themselves 'kingdom centred', while not denying, of course, the action of Christ and the Spirit outside the Church's visible boundaries. This leads it to emphasise the indissoluble relationship between Christ, the kingdom and the Church.[44]

The effect of this strong emphasis is to downplay how the kingdom can be understood to be present among peoples outside the visible Church, present, indeed, in the hearts of men and women who follow other religious paths.[45]

It is also to downplay these words of Pope John Paul II: 'The Spirit's presence and activity affect not only the individuals but also society and history, peoples, cultures and religions.'[46] In his grand vision of how the Spirit vivifies collective and not just individual realities, Pope John Paul, while not declaring the non-Christian religions to be, *per se*, salvific structures (paralleling, so to speak, the indissolubly linked realities of kingdom, Christ and Church), has noted, nonetheless, that these religions contain graced elements, have structures that mediate truth, and so, by implication at least, are in a position to offer something that Christians can find enriching. *Dominus Jesus* has a decidedly different tone and emphasis, saying:

> If it is true that the followers of other religions can receive divine grace, it is also certain that, *objectively speaking* they are in a gravely deficient situation in comparison with those who, in the Church, have the fullness of the means of salvation.[47]

So, Joseph Ratzinger's emphasis, certainly in *Dominus Jesus*, is not quite that of John Paul II. Hence, perhaps, the remark of Seattle's archbishop, Alexander Brunett: 'those who know well the thinking of John Paul II will recognize that this declaration does not add to the dialogue process.'[48]

Neither the present Pope nor his predecessor takes the route of interpreting the silence of Vatican II on whether the non-Christian religions are, *per se*, vehicles of salvation as leaving that question open to affirmation. Gavin D'Costa interprets Vatican II's silence as not really leaving the question open, but as, basically, saying no to it.[49] He is aware that various post-conciliar theologians have interpreted this differently, saying of them: 'These theologians tend to envisage a very close relationship between nature and grace.'[50] The ones who envisage a much sharper distinction between nature and grace – D'Costa includes John Paul II here and I would, decidedly, add Joseph Ratzinger – are clear in affirming that the non-Christian religions cannot, *per se*, be salvific structures and that to declare them to be so would amount to christological and ecclesiological relativism. We have seen all that.

It could be interesting at this point to explore whether according salvific status to non-Christian religions would *necessarily* involve us in christological and ecclesiological relativism; but such an exploration would bring us wide of where Ratzinger would wish us to go.

In his 2007 book on Christology, theologian Benedict XVI reveals much about his understanding of inter-religious dialogue. He is close to the approach to dialogue of Rabbi Jacob Neusner, because Neusner, just like Joseph Ratzinger himself, places the question of *truth* unashamedly at the core of his approach to inter-religious dialogue.[51] I am perplexed when I hear people saying, with surprise, that Ratzinger's openness to and appreciation of Neusner's approach is touching – dialogical beyond what they would have expected from him. It is in no way surprising, for Ratzinger and Neusner are in fundamental agreement as to what dialogue is about; it is about *truth*. Neusner would not have become a follower of Jesus as a result of hearing the Sermon on the Mount, he says, precisely because he recognised the kinds of claims that Jesus was making – truth claims that Neusner, as a faithful Jew, could not accept – and so he could not follow.[52] Benedict XVI understands this perfectly. In dialogue among the religions, truth must not be jettisoned; and he does not expect others to jettison it either.

To sum up: in a move not untypical of Ratzinger, once he has made his point with vigour, he shows himself not to be completely without understanding with regard to the relativism of our times – and he does so in more areas than the one that we have only had space to explore here: inter-religious dialogue. He is clearly in sympathy with the general impulse that goes hand in hand with the democratic ideal of according freedom of speech and freedom of worship to all and he is conscious, also, of how this impulse is best honoured when we express our truth in love, in a manner that is considerate towards our fellow human beings. Indeed, aware that too readily claiming truth can lead to an authoritarianism, at times even to a kind of absolutism, he says that 'a certain circumspection with regard to any claim to truth is entirely appropriate;'[53] but abandoning all claims to truth is not!

A Fleeting Glance at Moral Relativism

In the contemporary (postmodern) sceptical age, Ratzinger sees the doctrine of *objective values* as being challenged also by the prevailing relativistic mentality. In a previous chapter, it was seen how he understood the doing of things to be rooted in the being of things – so this does not have to be repeated here.[54] However, it is necessary to highlight his concern about how, in a relativistic climate, values tend to be made relative to the whims and desires of individuals. In his 1996 interview, *Salt of the Earth*, when pointing out that there are 'givens' that come with our being created – that not all is a matter of our inventing – he says:

> The idea that 'nature' has something to say is no longer admissible; man is to have the liberty to remodel himself at will.[55]

Ratzinger's Platonic emphasis with regard to humanity – that the 'idea' human being precedes each created human being – ensures that we not be thought of as blind products of chance but rather as God's 'project', receiving who and what we are from God's creating love. And it is this – this which is received – that norms/ guides how *we* are to live. Here is a doctrine of objective values, a strong '*logos*-precedes-*ethos*' emphasis. This emphasis on how values are discovered, not invented, leads to less of a focus being put on action or praxis, or on human beings' concrete historical experience, in the formulation of ethical positions. In the contemporary relativistic climate that so preoccupies him, Ratzinger is careful not to give hostages to history, situation or community, lest a relativism of values might detract from what are *true* values that, in a real (Platonic) sense 'precede' us. He views the struggle with relativism as having its roots in the contemporary ubiquity of plurality. So he sets out, in the area of morality too, to counter the prevailing relativism. He is not always unopposed, even in Catholic circles.

An Italian Catholic philosophy professor, Dario Antiseri, who characterises himself as an obedient Catholic, disagrees with Ratzinger in relation to natural law, relativism and nihilism. Antiseri notes the pluralism of our ethical conceptions. He asserts that 'an eye for an eye,' and 'love your neighbour as yourself' are very different principles, asking if we have a *rational* criterion for deciding between them. He thinks not, reminding us of Pascal. Pascal saw that we have no rational criterion for determining what is just or unjust. Our reason is not the gateway for morality; faith is. Faith as gift – preached, proposed, listened to – is that gateway. We can know the truly good only by means of revelation.

Here can be found a positive meaning for 'relativism,' for it is nothing other than the recognition that we cannot ourselves come up with what is definitive. Antiseri argues that even nihilism can be defended – as 'the regaining of room for the sacred.' As for natural law? Antiseri is sceptical. Why? Because human reason, he says, can not reach at all, in a forthright manner, what faith enables us to state with confidence.[56]

I am not so sympathetic to Antiseri's 'heart has its reasons', somewhat fideistic approach to ethics that then allows him to affirm relativism understood as a relativising of all conflicting ethical positions. Here, somewhere, there is a downgrading of the created gift of reason and, even, a sliding towards a certain nihilism with regard to our capacity to recognise, to discover, true values. But it is not uninteresting that a Catholic philosophy professor registers disagreement with Ratzinger – now Benedict indeed – in regard to the spectre of relativism.

A more interesting, more practical, challenge to Joseph Ratzinger's facility for denouncing a 'relativism' construed in a purist, ahistorical, 'ism'-like manner, was penned by Austin Dacey in the *New York Times* (March 2, 2006). Dacey argued that, between 'absolute moral values' and a relativism of the 'all values are equal' variety, there is a sizeable grey area, at least when one considers *how we actually operate*. Ethicists, he pointed out, distinguish between defeasible and indefeasible moral claims. The former are good rules of thumb; but they can be countered or overruled for countervailing moral reasons. For example, the rule of thumb that one should not lie is a good one, but one could have an obligation to lie if, by doing so, it protected the life of a person. Or, Dacey wrote, suppose you find that you cannot be absolute because you are conscious of an uncertainty, a fallibility even, and you recall having had to sincerely revise (relativise?) beliefs before in the light of new information? Dacey's point: hesitancy, and a certain relativising, can be quite appropriate when one recognises the presence of a genuine uncertainty.

It has to be admitted that Dacey's points might not completely convince, if taken just one by one; yet most of us know that we have had, concretely, to relativise (in his sense) this or that moral standard for good reasons, and maybe even to do greater good. I will leave it there.

The point is that, in response to Ratzinger's hard-hitting statements against contemporary relativistic inclinations, there are people whom he is provoking into thought, people who remind us, maybe, that it is one thing to assert the existence of absolute moral values but that it is another to bring these to bear on life-situations in (at least some) contemporary cultural contexts. Often Ratzinger's views seem to take these complexities but scantily into account. It is the old business of the essentialist at odds with the concrete-historicalist! Since he has become Benedict XVI he has provoked more reactions at *various* levels – not only theological, but also both philosophical and journalistic, as has just been seen – and, while the conversations may not come to full *quaestiones disputatae* in a formal sense, dispute and controversy nevertheless remain possible, even likely.

8

EUROPE

Introductory Remarks:
Europe a Continent in Crisis

Joseph Ratzinger is distressed about Europe. In his view, it has lost hope in its ability to become anything substantial and is dogged by a strange lack of confidence both about its past and about its future. This loss of confidence manifests itself in a hollowing out, 'a crisis of its circulatory system' and a lack of desire for life, for a future, even for children, as well as in a weariness about its own religious tradition, to which it refuses to appeal in the task of constructing a way forward.[1] The European way of life – universalised in 'the ideal of a world shaped by technology and material comforts' – has, to an extent, precipitated similar crises in other societies also with regard to their religious traditions.[2] And yet, whereas Europe has become entirely unconfident about being able to retrieve a spiritual basis for people's lives from its own religious heritage – Ratzinger speaks of 'a basis that seems to have slipped out of the hands of old Europe'[3] – others are finding a renewed confidence that their religious traditions can offer just such a basis: Muslims in several Islamic countries, for example, as well as peoples inspired by the religious traditions of Asia, particularly the mystical element of these that is expressed in Buddhism.[4]

About Europe, then, some searching reflection is required; and Ratzinger has provided much of it over his many years of writing. First of all, he has examined the various heritages of Europe and attempted to highlight the distinctive factors that have shaped its character but that seem, strangely, to be eclipsed today. Secondly, he has undertaken a diagnosis and analysis of Europe's present-day condition in an effort to understand why it reels with a kind of death-wish, waiting for its end to arrive instead of providing that service to others that they may surely expect from a continent that possesses such a rich heritage[5] Finally, he has probed what the way forward might be, out of the current impasse, for a Europe whose people ('we Europeans') still carry 'a great responsibility for the humanity of today'[6] Thus Joseph Ratzinger has reflected on Europe's past, its present, and its future.

I propose here to follow this same path, drawing, for the past, mainly, but not solely, on his writings about Europe in the period approximately from 1978 to 1992. With regard to the present and the future, Ratzinger's more recent writings – those penned in the first decade of the twenty-first century – will be the chief focus of inquiry. These latter were occasioned in the main by important speaking engagements to which he was invited. At the end of the chapter, a few critical reflections will be offered concerning Ratzinger's ideas about Europe.

Europe's Past: A Heritage That Obliges

In his earlier period of writing about Europe,[7] Ratzinger draws attention to four main heritages that have made Europe what it is: the Greek; the heritage of the Christian East; that of the Latin West; and the heritage of the modern period.[8] He indicates how each, in its own way, provides for, indeed embodies, the mutual ordering of faith and reason. The Greek heritage distinguishes between goods and the good, pointing thereby to a standard or measure beyond this or that particular good and thus implying a rule of law that finds its basis in criteria that transcend what the law, on its own, can give itself. Thus, in the (many) meanings that the Greeks (and our own times) give to 'democracy', it is – in its Platonic sense, anyway – always linked to *eunomia,* to the validity of truly good law that is based on moral criteria and not simply on the interests of the majority. In fact, majorities, too, are bound by such law. What this implies is that law /reason and religion/faith, while they remain distinct, may never be completely separated from one another, since it is from moral criteria (found in the domain of religion/faith/values) that the rule of law (formulated in the domain of reason) ultimately finds the foundation that it is incapable of providing for itself.[9]

The early Christian heritage – the heritage, that is, of the Christian East – is best elucidated by reference to one of Ratzinger's favourite New Testament texts: Acts 16:9. Here the Macedonian appeals to Paul: 'Come over to Macedonia and help us'; and in his appeal, Paul hears God calling early Christian faith to cross the narrow strip of sea to Macedonia, which stands for Greece, for Europe, so that a synthesis can be achieved between this faith and Greek rationality.[10] Reflecting on all this, Ratzinger notes that 'Christianity is the synthesis mediated in Jesus Christ between the faith of Israel and the Greek spirit.'[11] And from this encounter between Greek rationality and early Christian faith, given expression in Acts 16:9 in which the Macedonian, who stands for the Greek spirit, says to Paul, the embodiment of early Christian faith, 'come over to Macedonia and help us,' the reality of Europe is born:

> In its highest purification, the Greek spirit had become a desire for Christ, an open vessel held out towards the gospel of Jesus Christ. Europe became Europe through the Christian faith, which carries the heritage of Israel in itself, but at the same time has absorbed the best of the Greek and Roman spirit into itself.[12]

Europe in a profound way embodies a unity between reason and faith that is severed only at peril of falsifying its true Christian heritage. The implication is that Europe will be a social order in which reason is broadened, comes to itself, in its links to faith. This order will acknowledge God, and Christian values, in a public way, not relegating what is religious to the private, subjective sphere; and in this way it will ensure *eunomia* is its basis as genuinely 'good law based on recognized moral criteria and respect for a higher authority.'[13]

The Latin heritage of Christianity – it may be called the 'Christian West' – refers to that period in Europe's history when it more or less became synonymous with the area of the Latin culture and Church.[14] This area was extensive, including not only those who spoke Romance languages, but also Teutonic, Anglo-Saxon and some Slavic peoples (especially Poles).[15] It was the *res publica christiana* and 'not any politically constituted structure but a real and living totality in the unity of civilization.'[16] With its nation-transcending legal systems, universities, councils, its established and widely spread religious orders, and its lively embeddedness within the Church's spiritual life, centered on Rome, this *res publica christiana* signified the continued overcoming of the nationalistic principle and the creation of a space in which different peoples, living together, could be respectful of one another because each was respectful, in a common faith, of that which lay over all of them.[17]

Ratzinger sees that the *res publica christiana* had its limitations – it was too narrowly Latin and Western and it lacked the appropriate distinction between law and faith, state and Church, that we later came to value through the gains of the modern period – but he considers that we would be saying goodbye to Europe if we abandoned it entirely as a heritage.[18] The strength of this conviction of his is borne out in what he said in his 1980 homily, *Wahrer Friede und wahre Kultur*:

> Every European people may and must confess that it was the faith that created our home and that we would lose ourselves if we threw away the faith.[19]

Finally, the modern (or Enlightenment) heritage embodies what Ratzinger calls 'essential and indispensable dimensions of the European idea' that need to be adopted: 'the relative separation of state and Church, freedom of conscience, human rights and the independent responsibility of reason.'[20] The Enlightenment drew attention, at a time when 'the voice of reason had been too much tamed,' to Christianity's original appreciation of the rational element, so that reason was given back its own voice.[21] This proved invaluable insofar as reason did not lose its foundations in respect for God and for fundamental Christian moral values, but increasingly valueless – and anti-European – insofar as reason's independence got pushed to levels of emancipation and autonomy that severed it from its orientation to faith and to the religious traditions of humanity.[22] At its best, the Enlightenment made possible what Ratzinger calls 'a fruitful dualism of state and Church' in tandem with fundamental Christian humane values supporting, indeed implying, *inter alia*, a pluralist democracy for Europe, built on its own non-relativistic kernel.[23] That is a heritage to be preserved, for in it reason receives from faith what it cannot give itself, while at the same retaining its appropriate autonomy.

Europe's Present:
A Continent Out of Kilter with Itself

From reflection on how Ratzinger has spoken about Europe's main heritages, hints have already become available as to how he views the current situation of the continent. He sees it as having strayed from the identity embodied in its heritages. It has capitulated increasingly to a radicalized form of reason – and freedom – that has become severed from Europe's Christian foundations. Thus Europe, having bought into an autonomous reason that is honed to the strictest Enlightenment demands – but that in reality betrays the best of the Enlightenment heritage – has more and more become a continent seeking to shape human affairs in a way that completely excludes God and that 'leads us ever closer to the edge of the abyss, to the total abolition of man.'[24]

Today, Joseph Ratzinger says, there exist 'the two great cultures of the West, that is, the culture of the Christian faith and that of secular rationality,' and, while neither can be said to be universal, they are 'an important contributory factor (each in its own way) throughout the world and in all cultures.'[25] The former did not begin in Europe, but it did acquire, in that continent, 'its most historically influential cultural and intellectual form.'[26] The latter developed in Europe in the wake of the form of scientific rationality that came with the Enlightenment.[27] Despite both cultures being rooted in Europe, they are in fundamental opposition to one another. The former recognises the fact of Europe's Christian history, roots and character; the latter, although it found its starting-point in Christian Europe, is now inimical to Christian faith and embodies a radicalisation of the Enlightenment that takes it beyond what is genuinely European to the construction of a post-European phenomenon (and hence society) that is silent on God and has abandoned its Christian roots.[28] Ratzinger speaks of this second culture as

> a culture that, in a way hitherto unknown to humanity, excludes God from public consciousness, whether he is totally denied or whether his existence is judged to be indemonstrable, uncertain, and so is relegated to the domain of subjective choices, as something in any case irrelevant for public life.[29]

This culture, deemed 'post-European' by Ratzinger because it rejects Europe's identity as a society 'based on Christian culture,'[30] made its presence felt in the recent opposition in Europe to mentioning God – or the Christian roots of Europe – in the (attempted) draft European Constitution.[31] This exclusion, based, it is often argued, on the wish to be open to Europe's present-day multi-culturalism, is mistaken, making Europe's draft Constitution markedly different, for example, from the admirable constitution of the Federal Republic of Germany, after the Berlin Wall fell.[32] It shocks rather than appears simply 'as tolerance' to believers from elsewhere – Muslims and others – since none of these has sought to exclude God and the sacred from every area of public life in the way that Europe has, in an astonishing infidelity to its heritage.[33] This infidelity brings Europe's very survival into question:

Here we notice a self-hatred in the Western world that is strange and that can be considered pathological; yes, the West is making a praiseworthy attempt to be completely open to foreign values, but it no longer loves itself; from now on it sees in its own history only what is blameworthy and destructive, whereas it is no longer capable of perceiving what is great and pure. In order to survive, Europe needs a new – and certainly a critical and humble – acceptance of itself, that is, if it *wants* to survive. Multiculturalism, which is continually and passionately encouraged and promoted, is sometimes little more than the abandonment and denial of what is one's own, flight from one's own heritage. But multiculturalism cannot exist without shared constants, without points of reference based on one's own values. It surely cannot exist without respect for what is sacred. Part of it is approaching with respect the things that are sacred to others, but we can do this only if what is sacred, God himself, is not foreign to us.[34]

The radical Enlightenment conception of reason as absolutely independent and autonomous seems, at first glance, to offer enormous freedom to people. After all, they can now think as they like, freed from the constrictions of religion;[35] and this makes reason appear to have greater breadth. But the opposite is the case. Reason is reduced, not broadened, here, becoming purely scientific, positive, experimental reason. It is narrowed to a reason that is incapable of taking any cognisance of God, that is confined to pure *ratio* and deprived of the profound activities belonging to *intellectus*, and that is pitiably incomplete, having lost its cultural roots and abandoned its ties to the historical memory of humanity.[36] Such 'an exclusive reliance on technological reason and its possibilities' leaves reason impoverished and weak – no longer daring truth – and thus inhospitable to God and to the values associated with belief in him.[37] Its price is high: it makes for a Europe out of kilter with itself because the true identity of Europe is that it embodies a synthesis between reason and faith, not their absolute separation. But this authentic European heritage is collapsing today; and that is the crisis that Europe faces.

Further evidence for Europe's current state of crisis can be found in its rapidly declining birth rate, which testifies decisively to its lack of belief in, and desire for, a future.[38] Also, there is the fact that the Koran, or the beliefs of Judaism, command and receive the respect they rightly deserve while, at the very same time, Jesus Christ and everything about him are sidelined in the name of a questionable freedom.[39] This freedom, wishing to avoid intolerance at all costs, ends up, as was hinted at above, becoming strangely contradictory of itself and exemplifying the tyranny – indeed, paradoxically, the intolerance – of a political correctness that, in declaring all things equal, deprives that which is one's own (namely, Europe's Christian heritage) of any inclusion or expression at all.[40] Of such political correctness, Ratzinger says that it enshrines 'a single way of thinking and speaking,' prescribing this as the only way to be fashionable and deeming those who uphold traditional values intolerant.[41]

The freedom that allegedly comes with the culture that claims freedom from God and the Christian roots of Europe is no freedom at all. With reason cut off from its roots, there remains no compass to steer by, so human beings become the measure of their own action. This may be freedom, but it is an empty, negative, directionless kind.[42] Anything we can do, we may do; otherwise freedom, the 'supreme, absolute value,' is violated.[43] But what kind of freedom is this, when the measure of ourselves knows no standard beyond ourselves? The idea of freedom embodied in the radical, rationalist, autonomous culture that has developed in Europe is one that cannot co-exist with God's existence, since God is viewed as a limiting, all-seeing supervisor, a competitor, an enslaver, rather than as one whose glance saves.[44] Thus Europe's newer, second culture rejects God and the Christian roots of Europe in order to possess a freedom that, like the absolute reason that holds sway in the same culture, has lost its orientation to values and to truth; it has lost God. To Ratzinger this disastrous situation cries out for a response.

Europe's Future:
A Heritage Retrieved and Developed

Europe's peoples – above all, but by no means exclusively, Europe's Christians as committed, creative minorities[45] – are called on by Ratzinger to have confidence in their inheritance to give life again to the soul of Europe and to provide for it a future that it is now denying itself. So he makes a daring proposal. In the heyday of Europe's Enlightenment, he says, when people were asked to live as if there was no God, as if reason alone were the measure of all things, this was possible because at that time belief in God was still a prevalent force (indeed at that time faith stood to benefit from the rediscovery of the rational element). Today, however, with autonomous reason being taken ever more as the measure of all things, he proposes to reverse the Enlightenment's *as if*. He asks people – not only Christians and lapsed Christians (as might have been his earlier focus) but indeed even non-believers ('we Europeans')[46] – to live as if God existed, to live as if there were a higher authority and a measure of things that stood above the capacities of reason alone.[47] In a world where acknowledgement of the sacred and public recognition of God have diminished almost to zero, the challenge to live as if God existed acquires new urgency, indeed necessity – if Europe is not to lose its soul. To live as if God existed would be a kind of modern-day adopting of Pascal's famous wager and would be a step towards responding to the spiritual emptiness that Ratzinger witnesses in contemporary European culture, which in fact is no longer truly European.

From all that he has written, it is evident that Ratzinger regards Europe as much more than an economic, political or legal community. It constitutes, for its citizens, an entire living space, a way of being together by different peoples that is founded on a mutual ordering of faith and reason. And this mutual ordering of faith and reason is the real spiritual foundation on which authentic European culture rests and that marks what Europe really is. Social arrangements, even if they arise in the geographical space that is Europe today, are not authentically European if they lack

117

this mutual ordering.[48] Indeed this ordering acts as a criterion for discerning what is authentically European and what is not. Thus Europe's future cannot be constructed arbitrarily and still be authentically European. Its essence now provides a blueprint for its own future shaping and development.

About this 'essentialistic' thrust in Ratzinger's writings on Europe, some critical remarks will be made in the next and final section of the chapter. For the moment, it is interesting to note that, in his more recent writings on Europe, his focus is not so much on discerning Europe's core identity through examining its history, although he has not ceased to be concerned with this,[49] but rather on 'the criteria for correct political action against the background of the present European and global situation.'[50] The situation of Europe today demands this change of focus; Europe's identity as centred on the mutual ordering of faith and reason cannot continue to be set aside. Australian theologian Tracey Rowland put it:

> From Benedict's perspective the suicide of the West began when people stopped believing in the Christian account of creation and started to sever the intrinsic relationship between faith and reason.[51]

The result of this severance is the soulless, jaded Europe mentioned already in our introductory remarks as a Europe that distresses Ratzinger by lacking an orientation to life and to a future; it is a Europe that, in getting rid of God, has managed to get rid of humanity as well.[52] Ratzinger calls on this Europe, currently characterised by an abyss-like divide between its two cultural heritages, to recover the heritage of faith that would bring the 'know-how' achievement of Enlightenment reason up to speed with the moral heritage of Christianity.[53] At the moment Europe's two cultures, the most significant players in the world,[54] have parted ways, and they need to be put together again. Thus Ratzinger calls on contemporary Christians to help to redeem reason and to restore God to the picture:

And so it is plain that Christians today face a great challenge. Their task and ours is to see to it that reason is fully functional, not just in the realm of technology and material progress in the world, but also and especially as a faculty of truth, promoting its capacity to recognize what is good, which is a necessary condition for law and therefore also a prerequisite for peace in the world. Our task as contemporary Christians is to make sure that our idea of God is not excluded from the debate about man.[55]

In the end, Ratzinger is asking for a restoration of faith's vision of things, which, because it knows that God is *Logos* and is Love,[56] is able to trust in the creative power of a reason – and in the moral goodness of a freedom – that remain in relationship with God. Europe today needs people who do not fear that the glance of God destroys their reason and their freedom, but who witness rather to the happiness of Christian lives that are lived in mindfulness of God's look of love, which preserves the fullness of their truth and is the ultimate guarantee of their dignity.[57] Europe today needs people – and here Ratzinger refers once again to 'creative minorities' – who can demonstrate the attractiveness, the greatness, of the Christian model of life.[58] It needs Christians who are ready to engage scientists and philosophers on 'the basic question of what makes the world cohere.'[59] It needs the positive witness of Christians if it is to have confidence to re-engage with its own Christian heritage and roots. It needs people 'who make God visible in this world through their enlightened and lived faith,' people like Benedict of Nursia; for God returns among people only through people touched by God.[60] If this can happen, Europe's Christian roots will become accessible again, and God – and the morality associated with God – will be sidelined no longer, but seen to be essential to public life and indispensable for the task of building the Europe of tomorrow.[61]

Some Critical Reflections

With typical incisiveness, Joseph Ratzinger seeks to identify the maladies of contemporary Europe and to awaken it to the challenges that it faces if it is to survive and build a meaningful future that is faithful to its heritage. Consistent with his well-known view that the preaching of the Gospel far exceeds a mere clothing of it in the fashions and thought-patterns of the culture, he envisages the Gospel as 'a slit' or a 'cut' that incises the culture, purifying it so that the impurities within it are bled out and its elements of potential are enabled to ripen. This process is a painstaking one.[62] In it, the 'pathologies of reason' and 'pathologies of religion' that belong to that more recent, radical Enlightenment culture that has grown up in Europe are identified and vigorously pursued in a manner that challenges our ideas of reason and freedom to discard their absolutist claims, retaining instead the breadth and direction that faith in God gives them and that they cannot ever confer upon themselves.

I can affirm much of this; there is no doubt that the dialectical Joseph Ratzinger has an eye for what is debilitating and is relentless in exposing it. However, what he proposes must itself be subjected to a theological critique. Many writers have attempted this, most notably in relation to how Ratzinger speaks about Europe in terms of a core identity. He has a clear idea of what Europe is – and is not – and seeks to specify its future on the basis of that. But others find this approach too restrictive, too inclined to exclusivism, even too dangerous.

Werner Jeanrond, although without referring to Ratzinger's views on the Christian character of Europe, argues against what he calls 'the myth of a Christian Europe.'[63] He does not conceive Europe as an 'identity' or 'idea' or 'essence'; rather, he speaks about the project of European integration, saying that it should, first of all, be understood in legal, and not in religious, terms: 'The European Union constitutes a community of law, and not a community of views of life.'[64] Later, he speaks of Europe as 'a space where people of different religious and secular orientations and backgrounds attempt to live together in closer co-operation.'[65] But as regards this living together his focus is more on the actual provisions that make it work rather than on some 'identity' that would integrate it in an overall sense. He is cautious about focusing too sharply on the Christian identity of Europe, saying: 'References to "identity" are always problematic in that they often carry some claim to unity and uniformity.'[66] They are not the most helpful if one is seeking to build a future, pluralist Europe.[67]

A somewhat similar caution about speaking of 'identity' is found in Gillian Wylie, who writes that the European Union 'is not an entity currently based on a widely shared identity (despite the ardent hopes of its founders and today's Europhiles) but on shared values, political structures and economic ties.'[68]

An ambiguity is evident here in some of the ways in which 'Europe' is spoken about, since at times it is obvious that what is meant is the 'European Union' – this is clearest in Wylie's case – but at times it appears to signify something more: a legally supported space in which diverse peoples live together cooperatively (W. Jean-rond); or: 'a cultural and historical concept' (J. Ratzinger).[69] With Ratzinger, whose 'identity' emphasis is found problematic by both Wylie (explicitly) and Jeanrond (implicitly), the fear is that such an emphasis can all too easily become an excluding one; there are many more people in Europe than Christians.[70] Hence Jeanrond's unease with 'the myth of a Christian Europe' and his reluctance to envisage the future of Europe in too strongly Christian terms. Its future will be pluralist; that is already evident from its present.

Appealing too strongly to Christianity to integrate it overlooks its emerging character – which is not to say that Christianity has no role to play.[71] But Jeanrond envisages that role, instead, more along the lines of a developed praxis of love.[72] He suggests that, in a pluralist context, such a praxis of love will exhibit convincing ways of relating to and respecting the many forms of otherness that will be present. These ways might be more convincing, too, given Christianity's rather dominating, indeed at times destructive, role in the past. Jeanrond is much more conscious than Ratzinger of the mixed character of Europe's Christian history and points out that 'Christianity's record as a religion that promotes peace, love and understanding in Europe is ambiguous indeed.'[73]

Bernice Martin finds that Ratzinger, in reflecting on Europe and in characterising its crisis, identifies it too easily with the Christian heritage only and sees in this heritage a rather idealised view of what the Catholic Church has done and can do.[74] It is one thing to say (as Ratzinger does) that Europe should not be ashamed of the religious and moral heritage that made it great and that can provide it with spiritual foundations today; it is another, Martin believes, to make claims for this heritage in excess of the wrinkles of its history and without due recognition of Europe's other sources of value.[75]

I share some of these writers' unease about Ratzinger's idea of Europe. Even if one agrees with him about the undisputed historical role of the Christian faith in giving life to Europe,[76] nevertheless questions of an empirical and a practical nature have to be raised today when it comes to the concrete shaping of Europe as it is now – its laws and institutions – for a multicultural and growing plurality of peoples.

Furthermore, it must be asked: does Ratzinger's close identification of what is European and what is Christian run the risk of tending to see 'Christian Europe' as binding upon all – in a way that exceeds what it is legitimate to propose to them based on Europe's faith-heritage? I have, of course, no quibble with his pointing out that it is a 'historical fact' that Europe has Christian roots;[77] also, I note that he is quite aware that Christianity did not begin in Europe and so cannot claim to be a European religion;[78] yet I cannot help becoming a little nervous when he concludes from the fact 'that Christianity received its most historically influential cultural and intellectual form' in Europe that it 'therefore remains intertwined with Europe in a special way.'[79] I think: does this then mean that Europe must be intertwined in a special way with every other inculturation of Christian faith? My nervousness is that the intertwining of Christianity and Europe, as he speaks about it, can appear to mean that Europe's Christian experience becomes normative, somehow, for the wider world. As Australian theologian Tracey Roland, who is by no means a critic of Joseph Ratzinger, points out (following an acknowledgement that he is aware that the Greek component of the faith-reason synthesis that formed the Christian faith out of which Europe resulted[80] is not necessary for salvation):

> None the less, Ratzinger believes that the relationship of faith to human reason arose providentially from the junction of the Greek and Hebraic cultures. For him an understanding of this relationship is indispensable. This is the universal cultural patrimony of Catholics across the globe and its importance was also recognized in paragraph 72 of John Paul II's encyclical *Fides et Ratio*.[81]

It is difficult not to hear these words as suggesting that the European Christian experience is normative for Christian experience everywhere. Joseph Ratzinger is not particularly known for being a proponent of the empirical notion of 'culture'; and the matters just discussed offer little confidence that he approaches other cultures with the consciousness that God's providential plan, which *Fides et Ratio* saw 'guiding the Church down the paths of time and history'[82] is guiding it now towards a (providential also?) fruitful, new encounter with non-European cultures and religions. I do not find it difficult to accept, in broad outline, Ratzinger's holding that there needs to be a (European-like) mutual ordering of faith and reason guiding the practice of religion in any society[83] – for all religions and every use of reason can develop 'pathologies' if left unchecked – but he may need to take greater care that, when holding this kind of faith-reason ordering to be a universal element enjoined also upon other societies (and the religions practised in them), that he does not appear to suggest that there is no adequate Christianity outside its European cultural form.

Ratzinger, brought along by the issues of the times, is perhaps less Eurocentric, less demanding now, for European ways in Christianity, than he was in 1980, when he said: 'Every European people may and must confess that it was the faith that created our home and that we would lose ourselves if we threw away the faith.'[84] Still, one cannot help having the impression that, at given times, he more or less pushes for as much as he can get (just compare his earlier attitude to Turkish entry into the EU with his eventual change on that matter).

The question arises: why does he focus so much on the European roots of Christianity? Is he concerned to preserve European particularity because he believes that Christianity could never incarnate itself elsewhere with the same richness as it did when it combined the Hebraic and Greek element to give us, as he puts it, 'Europe in the narrower sense'?[85] Is there a kind of thinking here that suggests that Christianity's failing to survive in Europe will somehow mean its failing to survive at all? This kind of thinking would not be very hopeful in terms of Christianity's future. For should Christianity not in fact be able to incarnate fully in any place – in ways even beyond our current imagining? I have a slight suspicion here: that Ratzinger is sometimes concerned not only with the survival of Christianity, but also with its survival incorporating European elements that he might deem indispensable, or at least highly desirable (e.g. certain liturgical practices, particular kinds of music, current elements of Church organisation), but that might one day be less prominent in what would be a thoroughly inculturated Asian or African Christianity. In the end, Joseph Ratzinger might just be a little too European; but the Church's future, present evidence seems to suggest, will not be.

9

WISE CAUTIONS AND LEGITIMATE HOPES

In this, the final chapter in this book on the theological ideas of Joseph Ratzinger, I hope, without at all pretending to have covered every area of his theology,[1] to look to the future. I promise no wild speculation; everything, as will quickly become obvious, is mapped out by Ratzinger/Benedict XVI through the lens of continuity.

Vatican II: Continuity or Rupture?

Joseph Ratzinger likes to emphasise continuity and underlying identity, rather than *change*, when talking about the Church. In an interview with Vittorio Messori in 1985, twenty years after the Second Vatican Council ended, he said:

> There is no 'pre-' or 'post-' conciliar Church: there is but one, unique Church that walks the path toward the Lord, ever deepening and ever better understanding the treasure of faith that he himself has entrusted to her. There are no leaps in this history, there are no fractures, and there is no break in continuity. In no wise did the Council intend to introduce a temporal dichotomy in the Church.[2]

Following (and even during) the Council, Ratzinger points out, there emerged talk of a 'spirit of the Council' that was in reality an 'anti-spirit' envisaging the Council itself as a kind of point zero, with everything 'new' that followed it being in all cases better than everything 'old' that preceded it.[3] This viewpoint, as Ratzinger had stated ten years earlier in an inquiry into the reception of Vatican II, understood this 'conciliar spirit' to be still unattained; and it saw the Council's dogmatic texts as mere preludes to that 'spirit'. The Pastoral Constitution on the Church, *Gaudium et Spes*, was seen as the document that everything else was really preparing for, that text itself being understood 'as just the beginning of an unswerving course toward an ever greater union with what is called progress.[4] The attitude was: what the Council started with *Gaudium et Spes* is basically all that really matters.

Against this attitude, in its various manifestations, Ratzinger asserted himself repeatedly, insisting that to speak of a 'conciliar spirit' in this way was in reality to misunderstand both the intentions of the Council Fathers and the texts of the Council itself.[5] Ratzinger did not outlaw speaking about a 'spirit of the Council' (either in his 1975 or in his 1985 texts), but he did say, in 1985: 'The reading of the *letter* of the documents will enable us to discover their true *spirit*.[6] He was not advocating a 'restoration' in the sense of a 'going back', he said, but he was saying that the 'true' Council would only be rediscovered through a return to its texts.[7]

Those words may represent earlier days of sharp commentary, but the Ratzinger (now Benedict XVI) of today stands in marked continuity with them. In his Christmas 2005 address to the Roman Curia, occurring forty years after the closing of the Second Vatican Council, Benedict notes how, following the Council, 'two contrary hermeneutics' had come 'face to face and quarrelled with each other'.

One is 'a hermeneutic of discontinuity and rupture,' the other a 'hermeneutic of reform,' which he clarifies as 'renewal in the continuity of the one subject-Church which the Lord has given to us.'[8] Benedict refers to the former hermeneutic as having 'caused confusion;' the latter, he says, 'silently but more and more visibly, bore and is bearing fruit.'[9] Of the former, he says things that are highly reminiscent of his earlier remarks: that it risks a split between the pre-conciliar and post-conciliar Church and that it sees the texts of the Council as being so marked by compromises designed to ensure unanimity that they do not really express the true spirit of the Council, which 'is not to be found in these compromises but instead in the impulses towards the new that are contained in the texts.'[10] According to this hermeneutic, then, 'it would be necessary not to follow the texts of the Council but its spirit.'[11] But according to his own hermeneutic – that of 'reform' – it would be from a careful concentration on the texts of the Council that its true spirit would be revealed.

For the position espoused by Ratzinger there are supporters (not mentioned by himself), as also there are questioners (not mentioned by him either). The supporters, curial Archbishop Agostino Marchetto and influential Italian Cardinal Camillo Ruini, highlight the continuity of the documents of Vatican II with those of previous councils, indeed with Catholic tradition as a whole. They each refer to a statement of Pope John Paul II in 2000 to support their case: 'To read the council as if it marked a break with the past, while in fact it placed itself in the line of the faith of all times, is decidedly unacceptable.'[12]

However, Ruini goes further, targeting the five-volume, multi-translated history of the Council edited by Giuseppe Alberigo – and in the U.S. by Joseph A. Komonchak of The Catholic University of America[13] – 'as the principal and most influential creator of the incorrect understanding.'[14] It uses the category 'event' inappropriately, he believes, to indicate a rupture, a change from 'before' to 'after,' a new beginning, as a hermeneutical key to examine and understand the Council. Cardinal Ruini confidently argues that this hermeneutic is coming to an end,[15] which pleases him, although a spate of recent writing suggests that the situation is not quite as he would wish.[16]

The main spokespersons of the side pointed to by Ruini as using an incorrect hermeneutic are non-curial people: historians and academics, but not bishops. Editors Alberigo and Komonchak and Jesuit historian John W. O'Malley are the well-known names. The last, in particular, has been highlighting for a long time now how Vatican II was very much about *how* and not at all exclusively about *what*. It was about style, manner, and it was a revolution in *how* the Church was acting.[17] It exemplified, indeed, a different *way* of being Church, a way quite different from the Church at the time of Vatican I (1869-1870), for example. Vatican II avoided the anathematizing, adversarial language typical of Councils such as Vatican I and Trent (1545-1563).[18] Reading Giuseppe Alberigo's short, one volume account of Vatican II at the point where he deals with the intentions of Pope John in calling this Council makes clear that it was meant to be *pastoral* and to reach out to the world, not to hold off from it and condemn it.[19] The Council was meant to be different. Its treatments of all sorts of topics occurred in a dialogical, not confrontational, stance towards the world; and that was new. The Pope never intended this to *change* what the faith of the Church was in its substance – recall his famous remark indicating that the substance of the faith is one thing and the manner of its presentation another – but it would be difficult to argue that his repeated insistence on the *pastoral* character of the Council did not signify a marked shift in how he wished the Church to *be* through this event.

In order to foster an appreciation of the newness of Vatican II's style, its *how* (so to speak), John O'Malley simply highlights the Council's vocabulary. For it signified a revolution in communication style, employing an endless horizontal vocabulary that represented a huge change from the verticality of all that preceded it. According to him, Vatican II's discourse was focused on persuading and inviting. He lists the *horizontal-reciprocal* words: 'cooperation,' 'partnership,' 'collaboration' and, most significantly, 'dialogue' and 'collegiality;' the *friendship* words: 'human family;' the *humility* words: 'pilgrim' Church, 'servant;' the words indicating *change*: 'progress,' 'development,' 'evolution' (not at all static, 'definition' words!); the *interiority* words: 'joy' and 'hope,' 'grief' and 'anguish'. Overall, there is a staggeringly new vocabulary here, a different kind of ecclesial language. Surely it cannot have meant: 'no change or discontinuity.'[20]

O'Malley is clear (as is Alberigo): as well as fundamental continuity with the great tradition of the Church, we cannot blind ourselves to the discontinuities – with previous practices, teachings, even Councils.[21] Something did happen; do not try to say that it did not! In a long section of O'Malley's article, 'The Council and the Councils,' discontinuites are highlighted between Vatican II and the twenty councils that preceded it: discontinuities in: who was present, how things were done, and so on; discontinuities, also, in document genre, style, and even in theological method(s). I have no space here to look at these in detail, so O'Malley's summary at the end of his article must suffice:

> I will summarize in a simple litany some of the elements in the change in style of the Church indicated by the Council's vocabulary: from commands to invitations, from laws to ideals, from threats to persuasion, from co-ercion to conscience, from monologue to conversation, from ruling to serving, from withdrawn to integrated, from vertical and top-down to horizontal, from exclusion to inclusion, from hostility to friendship, from static to changing, from passive acceptance to active engage-ment, from prescriptive to principled, from defined to open-ended, from behaviour-modification to conversion of heart, from the dictates of law to the dictates of con-science, from external conformity to the joyful pursuit of holiness.[22]

When all of the above elements are taken in the aggregate, O'Malley says, they indicate a model of spirituality, indeed a shift in model of Church – and therefore a shift in how the Church should look and in how it should behave. Here is captured 'change,' the 'spirit of the council'; and it is *not* nothing.

So how, then, should we interpret the Council? We should do so, O'Malley says, according to the excellent six norms that were proposed by the Extraordinary Synod of 1985, twenty years after Vatican II ended, but with one norm added: a norm that takes into account discontinuity.[23]

I agree; it is unhistorical to overlook discontinuities. As a historian, O'Malley believes the picture must be balanced by paying due attention *also* to the discontinuities: 'When we do so, one thing at least becomes clear: the council *wanted* something to happen.'[24]

The fact is: the Alberigo/Komonchak/O'Malley hermeneutic takes into account, unambiguously, *both* continuities *and* discontinuities. I do not hear much of that in Ruini and Marchetto; but, nuanced as always, I do hear it in Benedict XVI – above all in his Chrismas 2005 remarks. There, while favouring, even lobbying for, a *continuity* hermeneutic, he moves gently to a position of including also discontinuity while emphasising underlying continuity, in a nuanced espousal of what is presented as a 'hermeneutic of reform'.[25] So, Benedict XVI *does* acknowledge discontinuity, albeit in his own way. O'Malley embraces a hermeneutic of continuity *and* discontinuity, as do Alberigo/Komonchak, who do not speak unnuancedly of discontinuity, 'event', change, and so on, in the manner suggested, for example, by Marchetto and Ruini.[26] Benedict, in 2005, does not mention names on the Alberigo/O'Malley side. But when, following a reflection on 'three circles of questions' that had formed and were in need of an answer at the time of Vatican II,[27] he speaks as follows, no one can doubt that he has in mind that emphasis on discontinuities that marks *also* the hermeneutical approach of the side he does not favour. Benedict states:

> It is clear that in all these sectors, which all together form a single problem, some kind of discontinuity might emerge. Indeed, a discontinuity had been revealed but in which, after the various distinctions between concrete historical situations and their requirements had been made, the continuity of principles proved not to have been abandoned. It is easy to miss this fact at a first glance.[28]

Note here how a subtler Ratzinger/Benedict acknowledges discontinuity, then interprets it in terms of an ultimate continuity of *principles* – and then suggests that this could be missed 'at a first glance.' I find it difficult, however, to think of Alberigo, Komonchak and O'Malley (never mentioned by Benedict) as actually operating 'at a first glance'.

It is curious, nonetheless, how Benedict's reflections do admit of discontinuity after all, once he has found a way to incorporate that within an overall perspective of continuity. Continuing on from where he left off above, he says:

> It is precisely in this combination of continuity and dis-continuity at different levels that the very nature of true reform consists. In this process of innovation in continu-ity we must learn to understand more practically than before that the Church's decisions on contingent matters – for example, certain practical forms of liberalism or a free interpretation of the Bible – should necessarily be contingent themselves, precisely because they refer to a specific reality that is changeable in itself. It was neces-sary to learn to recognize that in these decisions it is only the principles that express the permanent aspect, since they remain as an undercurrent, motivating decisions from within.
>
> On the other hand, not so permanent are the practi-cal forms that depend on the historical situation and are therefore subject to change.[29]

Benedict XVI is astute. He has given something to the other side, while losing nothing from his own. His words echo those of Pope John XXIII about the substance of the faith remaining un-changed while the forms of its expression are updated.

It seems to me, however, that he interprets Pope John XXIII a bit differently from the Alberigo-O'Malley side, since Alberigo, arguing the newness in Pope John's *pastoral* emphasis and O'Malley, seeing the new *form* (the how, the style, the formal as opposed to the material element), actually argue that a massive change in form indicates significant discontinuity; nor do they make a continu-ity/discontinuity distinction in terms of *levels*. They highlight the change that comes with Vatican II; Ratzinger plays it down (without denying it completely). They accord a greater role to historical particularity, he a lesser. They are historians, he a dogmatic theologian. They are, first and foremost, in the field of Church history; he is, first and foremost, in the field of Church leadership.[30] And the context in which reflection is done is not insignificant for its emphases and conclusions.

The Significance of Benedict's Interpretation of Vatican II for his Unfolding Papacy

The interpretation favoured by Benedict XVI is proving significant for the direction that his papacy is taking. For his papacy, he said at its very beginning, he was not putting forward a programme of his own (though he was aware of the tasks that lay ahead of him).[31] Neither was his first encyclical, eight months later, the unveiling of a programme for his papacy.[32] Rather, suggests Irish moral theologian Raphael Gallagher, the context of that encyclical was the post-conciliar crisis of the Church in its struggle to interpret Vatican II correctly; and it is Benedict's desire that the Church should 'recuperate the proper intent of the Council Fathers'[33] and 'return to the roots of its Christian faith'[34] Gallagher made these points when writing on the second section of Benedict XVI's encyclical, *Deus Caritas Est.*[35]

I lean a little on his remarks here when speaking about what this papacy will bring. For the implication of these remarks is that speculations about the future of Benedict's papacy are more likely to be correct if the key *theological* concern from which the Pope operates – namely, to interpret Vatican II in continuity with previous councils and not as a kind of breach or novelty – is correctly identified. Benedict's own words confirm the absolute centrality of this concern:

> I too, as I start in the service that is proper to the Successor of Peter, wish to affirm with force my decided will to pursue the commitment to enact Vatican Council II, in

the wake of my predecessors and in faithful continuity with the millennia-old tradition of the Church.[36]

Raphael Gallagher's identification of the context of *Deus Caritas Est* as 'the tensions and controversies which have marked the reception of the Second Vatican Council within the church'[37] does not mean, it seems to me, that Benedict XVI lacks a programme of his own; for the Pope's interpretation of the Council and of change in the Church itself constitutes a decided programme that will influence very clearly what will happen during his papacy. Gallagher himself has indicated this by pointing to how Benedict is calling the Church, in the second part of the encyclical, to be visibly itself in the expression of *diakonia* (service of charity) no less than in the expressions of *kerygma* and *leitourgia*.[38] This is vintage Ratzinger: that *love* is the Church's mark, love that springs from the heart and is more than the requirements of justice, which is but a part of love.[39]

What he says here about the service of charity in the second part of *Deus Caritas Est* stands in continuity with: his earlier criticisms of *Gaudium et Spes*; his many cautions against an over-alignment of the Church with the world; and his notion of liberation theology as too set on 'making,' on fostering salvation through the building of just structures.

The theology of the relationship between faith and politics that is in *Deus Caritas Est* is in decided continuity with that which has been in the writings of Joseph Ratzinger over the previous thirty years. This theology views politics – and the developing of just structures – as the role of the state, with Christian faith's role being to purify/correct the thinking upon which the justice is based and, in its ecclesial presence, to present a service of charity to the world whose hallmark is love itself.[40] And it is a theology that he believes welds together the right way of conceiving the relationship between faith and politics and the right way of understanding Vatican II.

In other areas of ecclesial life, also, one can see how Ratzinger's theological positions and his hermeneutic of continuity in relation to the Second Vatican Council are inextricably interwoven. With regard to *liturgy*, for example, when responding to questions from priests of the diocese of Rome at the beginning of Lent 2006, he said:

> We must not overlook the common Catholic spirituality that is expressed in the liturgy and in the great tradition of the faith. This point is important, and it also concerns the Council. We must not live – as I said before Christmas to the Roman curia – the hermeneutic of discontinuity, but we must live the hermeneutic of renewal, which is the spirituality of continuity, of going forward in continuity. This also seems important to me in regard to the liturgy.[41]

A recent action of Benedict in relation to the liturgy can be seen to stem from his concern to interpret Vatican II in continuity with what preceded it. I have in mind his *motu proprio* on the Latin Mass. Avery Dulles, before ever the *motu proprio* appeared, had this to say:

> Ratzinger in several places laments the abruptness with which the Missal of Paul VI was imposed after the council, with its summary suppression of the so-called Tridentine Mass. This action contributed to the impression, all too widespread, that the council was a breach rather than a new stage in a continuous process of development. For his part, Ratzinger seems to have nothing against the celebration of Mass according to the missal that was in use before the council.[42]

My point here is: if one wants to understand what Benedict has done and is doing, and if one is interested in his likely future actions as Pope, one could employ as hermeneutical key – in every area of ecclesial life, not only in the examples that have been seen from the political and liturgical arenas – his concern to always interpret the documents of Vatican II in continuity with the councils that preceded it. *Continuity* is his lens, 'going forward in continuity.' He is suspicious of adding things to the faith, preferring to pare it back to its essentials. Journalist David Gibson put it this way in a recent book on him:

> Ratzinger's project was not to expand the interpretations of truth but to ensure that nothing was added to what existed at the beginning, to present the faith as it was, as it is, and as it always shall be. No filigree or self-indulgent imaginings should obscure the pure ideal.[43]

The hermeneutic of continuity is important to Benedict XVI with regard to all things, even himself. He sees himself as having been true, throughout his life, to a constant impulse: 'to free up the authentic kernel of the faith from encrustations and to give this kernel strength and dynamism.'[44] Accused in the 1980s of having changed, he responded: 'it is not I who have changed, but others.'[45] After his election as Pope, an article in the Jesuit magazine *America* suggested that he had been liberated by the papacy, freed to speak in a voice different from that of the Prefect of the CDF.[46] A late 2006 portrait of the new pope in *L'Espresso* magazine spoke similarly: 'He doesn't thunder condemnations, he doesn't hurl anathemas.'[47] But neither of these magazines suggested that any of this means a fundamental change in the man. When speaking to four German journalists before departing for his visit to his native Bavaria in September 2006, Benedict, when asked how he saw himself, said that he was 'happy that certain aspects that weren't noticed at first are now coming into the open' but that, in all that was essential he had 'remained identical.'[48]

I do not consider this self-assessment of Benedict to be a kind of illusion on his own part. He is in fact highly consistent. His changes – on such matters as episcopal conferences, increased freedom for theologians, communion (under carefully discerned conditions) for the divorced and remarried – can be attributed to changed historical circumstances that he saw as requiring him to change in order to stay the same.[49] Specific, identifiable changes do not necessarily indicate inconsistency. As Dulles says: 'Notwithstanding the changes, Benedict XVI has shown a fundamental consistency'[50] – a consistency of which he too is personally convinced.[51]

Looking Ahead:
Wise Cautions and Legitimate Hopes

Speaking about cautions and hopes can be tricky, for what prompts caution in one person may raise hope in another; and vice versa. I have just written at length about Ratzinger's continuity hermeneutic and about his remarkable self-consistency. Now the question arises: What is the import of these strong continuity emphases? Well, just as there is no striking discontinuity between the pre- and post-conciliar Ratzinger, neither will there be a striking discontinuity between Cardinal Ratzinger and Pope Benedict.

So I would caution those who are hoping for some fresh starts to temper their optimism. For even if change does come with Benedict – and I will argue that it will, mainly *vis à vis* the style of his predecessor – the emphasis with Ratzinger/Benedict will never be on change but on continuity. He has a strong trust in the Church's tried and tested methods (even when these are failing) and frequently calls for a 'return' to them in contexts that can dismay his hearers.

Recall his visit to Brazil from May 9-14 of 2007. His message centred on the need for a vigorous catechesis, a respecting of the liturgical norms, a social engagement along the lines of what is envisaged in *Deus Caritas Est* and a defence of funamental moral norms in a relativistic and consumerist culture. He also gave an account of the encounter of Christianity with the pre-Christian cultures of Latin America that illustrates that ecclesial hermeneutic of trust I mentioned above.[52]

One wonders if all this met, head on, the challenges to Brazilian Catholicism that Brazilian Cardinal Claudio Hummes (now head of the Congregation for the Clergy) was so exercised about before the visit and that led him to emphasise: 'The Church must respond today to the issues of today and not try to repeat what was done in the past.'[53] What Benedict brought to Brazil seems to me predictable, but not imaginative; on the flight there, he told reporters: 'I am not a specialist,' even as he recognised the importance of Latin America for the future of the Catholic Church.[54] The question must arise, then: what has his visit achieved with regard to that future?

Benedict's trips are relatively short; he goes, brings a message, and leaves. He is not focused on himself, but on clear essentials of the faith. Sometimes one wonders, however, if much is already *settled* in his mind, so that his travels, as living encounters, mean little. About nine months into his papacy, Paul Elie raised this word 'settled':

> Together John Paul II and Joseph Ratzinger carried out what Ratzinger declared the 'authentic interpretation' of Vatican II. As a result, in Rome today all the great Catholic controversies of the past half century – about women, sexuality, politics, and authority in the Church – are considered settled, and settled in the conservatives' favor. This gives Benedict a clear set of precedents and a staff of people who share his point of view. Yet it leaves him with less to do than the popes who preceded him. It means that his influence will most likely be felt more through his character than through his power to bring about change.[55]

Elie's words seem to me to be broadly correct. The lens of change will not be the one through which to view this papacy. A few months after he was elected, Pope Benedict said on Vatican Radio: 'My personal mission is not to issue many new documents, but to ensure that [John Paul's] documents are assimilated.'[56] Though he and John Paul II were very different in character, he believes they were one in relation to the many controversial questions handled by his Congregation (the CDF) during the 1980s and 1990s and that there is far less reason to rethink these than to implement them.

Speaking of the CDF, it seems to be operating in the present papacy along lines (and in pursuit of topics) more or less identical to those of the Prefect Ratzinger/Pope John Paul II era, except that the theology of its documents is inferior now to then. Its recent actions prompt me to issue wise cautions – rather than to express legitimate hopes – to theologians who are intrepid enough to write, still, in the contested (but vital) areas of liberation theology and theology of the religions (Jon Sobrino and Peter Phan). Furthermore, the CDF's recent decision to issue a document in large measure reiterating what was already clearly (and, as felt by many, offensively) taught in *Dominus Jesus* suggests, soberingly, that ecumenism in the West will continue to endure a wintry climate, even if a springtime is to be hoped for in relations with our Orthodox brothers and sisters. Cardinal Karl Lehmann, the head of the Catholic Church in Germany, recently questioned the appropriateness and deplored the negative ecumenical consequences of the CDF's issuing of that sequel document to *Dominus Jesus* on June 29, 2007, the publication of which Pope Benedict ordered.[57] The only change I see in the way the Congregation is proceeding in the present papacy is that the theologians judged to be questionable are not pursued with sanctions, as in the last papacy, although the pain of having one's Catholicity questioned is a severe enough sanction for most.

I had a different hope for theology under this pope. My hope had been that a theologian pope, well capable of making theology credible as a form of needed public discourse, would bring new life to the theological community worldwide. But despite Benedict's writing a book and inviting criticism of it by fair-minded readers (a revolution in papal style[58]), the CDF's continuing to act as it does has seen to the transformation of this legitimate hope into a wise caution.

If there are women reading these pages, they must wonder if they will be consulted any more in this papacy than they were in the last. I have been shocked, when reading the scholarly writings of Joseph Ratzinger over the years, at the extent to which the names of women are almost entirely absent from his footnotes, especially in view of their contribution to theological reflection in the last three decades or so. When asked recently about greater visibility and positions of higher responsibility for women in the Church (I am not talking here about ordination – the context was the fact of women's greater presence in departments of the Holy See today), Benedict's default position was to accept – seemingly as a matter of unchangeable fact, which it is not – canon law's limiting of the power to take legally binding decisions to sacred orders.[59]

Here is that unquestioning hermeneutic of trust again, that belief in the rightness of the way things are. Benedict seems never, in his context, to feel any need to question the Church's current arrangements and practices. Are they – despite the historical contingency of many of them – completely 'settled' also in his mind? He is aware of the tensions between Roman centralization and demands for strong, local episcopacies; he even espouses collegiality; yet, in the matter of how bishops are appointed, a process much in need of revision remains untouched. And this is not a question of doctrine.

Similarly, in the current context of a large decline in vocations to the priesthood, at least in certain parts of the world, will there, under him, be any examination of a structural or systemic nature regarding this decline and the problem accompanying it: the failure to provide the Eucharist for many believers? Any attempts to 'think outside the box' on this matter are unlikely to occur in Rome and, where they do occur, they will be unwelcome. The Dutch Dominicans have been ploughing a lonely furrow.[60]

The evangelizing outreach of Benedict will be more circumscribed than in the reign of Pope John Paul II, given the former's sparer (essentials of the faith) approach to evangelization[61] and the latter's mastery of gesture and media image. Also, Benedict seems to be more focused *ad intra* – on the community of the baptised – while the phenomenologist John Paul plumbed the world of wider human experience. The first two encyclicals of Benedict were addressed to the family of believers, not to the whole world. And Paul Elie has noted that 'the most consequential actions of his pontificate so far have all involved ecclesial matters.'[62] He is more Church-focused – consistent, maybe, with his 'mustard seed' approach to the Church of the future: leaner, but purer? Such narrowing makes me nervous, constrasting, as it does, with a remark once attributed to Cardinal Martini: if the people 'out there' do not come to us, then we must go to them.

Signs of Hope

I have been speaking essentially in cautioning terms. But did I not promise to speak of hopes also? Where might these be found? Not in Ratzinger's over-emphasis on continuity but perhaps in a discontinuity: the discontinuity between the papacies of John Paul II and Benedict XVI. Already many features stand out. Benedict sometimes wins people with his words, which are simpler (and fewer) than those of his predecessor. He remains 'a professor with an eye for precision and a pastoral touch,'[63] teaching at his Wednesday audiences, still meeting annually with his doctoral students, and finding time to show genuine hospitality to controversial figures such as Hans Küng. Pope John Paul II had not been able to bring to a conclusion the case of Fr Maciel, L.C. Benedict did so, dealing with the matter both compassionately and efficiently. Pope John Paul II related to crowds very differently to Benedict XVI; the latter discourages applause and any focus on his own person, being 'careful to direct attention to something beyond himself.'[64] Since he has become Pope, there have been significant changes in papal style (John O'Malley must surely be amused by this). And, if such 'discontinuities' are not nothing, as I believe, then his papacy may well achieve a verdict of the kind that John O'Malley gave to Vatican II: something *did* happen!

On the administrative front, Benedict is generally known to be more effective than John Paul II, so that things are getting done again in Rome – although hardly in sufficient dialogue with curial personnel. There is a certain bureaucratic tidiness – meetings begin and end on time – and this, even if stereotypically German (*Pünktlichkeit*), is welcome after the over-runs of the previous administration. On the doctrinal front, Pope Benedict has disappointed conservatives by not going on a witch-hunt, or thundering prohibitions – for example on his visit to Spain. On that visit, given that his time was very limited, he preferred rather to stress the point that 'Christianity, Catholicism, isn't a collection of prohibitions: It's a positive option.'[65] He tries to speak in warm, pastoral imagery, commending the faith by drawing attention to its inner beauty. As might be said in Ireland, he wants to show that Christianity is lovely. When a child spoke (using the familiar *Du*) of the problem of not being able to see God, Benedict spoke of not being able to see electricity either, or an idea one might have. He has a winning way with images and examples; yet he is anything but simple. Although not a lover of crowds and big media events, he seems to have worked out how he wants to be effective on the global stage, offering himself as a peacemaker, very much remininscent of his predecessor and namesake, Benedict XV.[66]

Benedict's changes are a matter of *style*, of *how*. But changes in style are always forerunners of deeper changes, opening new doors (like the ecological one). As journalist David Gibson pointed out in a book that preceded his Ratzinger volume, when presenting the argument of a number of bishops at the synod of 2001 to the effect that greater autonomy to local episcopacies and a strong pope were not incompatible:

> 'We need a strong pope as well as a strong episcopal college,' Belgium's Cardinal Godfried Danneels told the 2001 synod even as he argued for greater autonomy. Change in the church usually comes through a change in style, a shift in balance and emphasis – in how the church conveys the same old things to a new generation.
>
> Large-scale changes in Catholicism grow out of such minor adjustments. This has happened at various times in church history, and the last few decades have been such an era, even under John Paul. The Catholic Church holds the same firm beliefs that it did in the 1950s, but the church looks, acts, and sounds much different than it did before.[67]

The hopes, then, for those wishing for a more modest Church, centred on a core message, wishing to be quietly at the service of humanity by promoting peace, drawing attention to the beauty of Christian faith and reminding us of our responsibilties to care for one another and for the earth, are not inconsiderable. Benedict will keep these things before our eyes – in his own way, according to his rather unflamboyant, yet personable style. His *style* is his own; and that (in many ways contrary to his personal view but in accordance with the views of Cardinal Danneels, John O'Malley, and others) can make all the difference. It can – especially under Providence, and often invisibly – be a pointer to new ways of being Church, ways that are needed if Christian faith is to stand tall in a world that greatly needs it, ways perhaps that not even Benedict fully suspects.

NOTES

Introduction

1. This is the title given by *The Catholic Herald* (London) to a reflection I wrote following the publication of Pope Benedict XVI's first encyclical letter, *Deus Caritas Est.*

2. See Jim Corkery, S.J., 'On Christian Hope: the New Encyclical of Pope Benedict XVI', in Thinking Faith: the Online Journal of the British Jesuits, 18 January 2008. www.thinkingfaith.org/articles/20080118_5htm

3. See John W. O'Malley, *What Happened at Vatican II* (Cambridge MA, and London, England: The Belknap Press of Harvard University Press, 2008).

1. Origins: A Theologian Emerges

1. See 'Die Zukunft des Heils' in: Ulrich Hommes and Joseph Ratzinger, *Das Heil des Menschen. Innerweltlich-Christlich* (Munich: Kösel Verlag, 1975, pp. 31-63), p. 42.

2. See Cardinal Joseph Ratzinger. *'In the Beginning…': A Catholic Understanding of the Story of Creation and the Fall* (Edinburgh: T&T Clark, 1995 [original German 1986]), pp. 42-49.

3. See J. Ratzinger's commentary on theses 1-8 and 10-12 in *Quinze thèses sur l'unité de la foi et la pluralisme théologique* (Paris: C.L.D. Esprit et Vie, 1978, original German 1973), p. 12. Note the following sentence: 'La première question n'est pas: 'Qu'est-ce qui convient à notre époque?', mais: 'Comment la chose se présente-t-elle du point de vue de la foi?"

4. Homily at Mass 'Pro Eligendo Romano Pontifice', 18 April 2005 (consulted at www.vatican.va/gpII/documents/homily-pro-eligendo-pontifice_20050418_en.h… 13/12/2005).

5. Homily at Inauguration Mass of His Holiness Pope Benedict XVI, 24 April 2005 (consulted at www.vatican.va/holy_father/benedict_xvi/homilies/2005/documents/hf_ben-xvi… 12/12/2005).

6. See Joseph Kardinal Ratzinger, *Aus meinem Leben: Erinnerungen 1927-1977* (Munich: Wilhelm Heyne Verlag, 1998), pp. 21-23. The English translation is: *Milestones: Memoirs 1927-1977* (San Francisco: Ignatius Press, 1997).

7. *Ibid.*, see for example pp. 14-15.

8. *Ibid.*, see pp. 46-47.

9. *Ibid.*, p. 47.

10. *Ibid.*

11. *Ibid.*, see p. 49.

12. *Ibid.*, see pp. 49-50.

13. I suggest just one text here: '*Introduction to Christianity*: Yesterday, Today, and Tomorrow' in *Communio* 31 (2004): 481-495. In this Preface to the new German edition of his 1968 *Introduction to Christianity* in 2000, there are many 'enemies sighted' and there is much 'impassioned countering'.

14. For a contemporary cautioning against the optimism of this latter view, see Frederick Christian Bauerschmidt, 'Confessions of an Evangelical Catholic: Five Theses Related to Theological Anthropology' in *Communio* 31 (Spring 2004): 67-84 (here 70-74 in particular).

15. See Declan Marmion and Mary E. Hines, *The Cambridge Companion to Karl Rahner* (UK: Cambridge University Press, 2005), pp. 303-304.

16. Without lacking that critical, discerning perspective that is essential to any rounded theology, Timothy Radcliffe O.P. can be seen to embody more the 'detective of grace' approach. See '*The Tablet* Interview: An Enigma Wrapped in a Cowl', *The Tablet* (17/24 December 2005), pp. 8-9.

2. The Facial Features of a Theological *Corpus*

1. See J. Ratzinger, *Volk und Haus Gottes in Augustins Lehre von der Kirche* (People of God and House of God in Augustine's Doctrine of the Church). Munich: Karl Zink Verlag, 1954.

2. See Roberto Tura, 'La Teologia di J. Ratzinger: Saggio Introduttiva' in: *Studia Patavina* 21 (1974): 145-182, here 147; see also Aidan Nichols, O.P., *The Theology of Joseph Ratzinger: An Introductory Study* (Edinburgh: T & T Clark, 1988), especially chapter 2 and pp. 136-139 of chapter 7 (section entitled 'A eucharistic ecclesiology').

3. The eschatological interest is very early also, dating back to Ratzinger's *Habilitationsschrift* on Saint Bonaventure. See *The Theology of History in St. Bonaventure* (Chicago: Franciscan Herald Press, 1971 and 1989; original German 1959).

4. See, for example, in chronological order of appearance: Roberto Tura, 'La Teologia di J. Ratzinger', Jacques Rollet, *Le Cardinal Ratzinger et la Théologie Contemporaine* (Paris: Les Éditions du Cerf, 1987) and Aidan Nichols, O.P., *The Theology of Joseph Ratzinger*. (Since Ratzinger was elected pope last year a host of books have appeared, many of the more journalistic variety, a few of greater theological depth, but the studies I list are more substantial and have borne the test of time).

5. I reached this conclusion at the end of a doctoral dissertation on Ratz-

inger's theology. See James Corkery, *The Relationship between Human Existence and Christian Salvation in the Theology of Joseph Ratzinger* (Washington DC: The Catholic University of America, 1991), pages 494-500. Authorized facsimile available from University Microfilms International, Ann Arbor, Michigan, 1992. Others who note the consistency, or continuity, in Ratzinger's thought are: Michael A. Fahey, 'Joseph Ratzinger as Ecclesiologist and Pastor' in: *Concilium* 141 (January 1981): 76-83, here 76; also Joseph A. Komonchak, 'The Church in Crisis: Pope Benedict's Theological Vision' in: *Commonweal* 132:11 (June 3, 2005). (Following Pope Benedict's election, Fahey seems to pull back from his earlier view that Ratzinger's thought exhibits 'an amazing consistency'. For while it is true that, in his 1981 article, Fahey detected, in Ratzinger, 'a gloominess and depression about undesirable developments in the wake of the council', he did not interpret these mental states as signs that Ratzinger had changed, but rather as indicative of Ratzinger's view that others had changed the council's true meaning. Yet in 2005 Fahey said he had described Ratzinger's 'paradigm shift' in that earlier article. He spoke also in 2005 of Ratzinger having had 'an intellectual conversion.' But he did not speak thus in 1981. See Michael A. Fahey, 'Blessings on Pope Benedict XVI. From the Editor's Desk' in: *Theological Studies* 66 (June 2005): 251-252.

6. See J. Ratzinger, 'Sühne: V. Systematisch' in: *Lexikon für Theologie und Kirche* IX. Second Edition (1964): 1156-1158, here p. 1157. Also, see *Introduction to Christianity* (New York: The Seabury Press, 1969), p. 196; also p. 43.

7. 'Diventando sempre più un teologo sistematico nell' ottica agostiniana e bonaventuriana' (see R. Tura, 'La Teologia di J. Ratzinger', p. 145).

8. *Der Gott des Glaubens und der Gott der Philosophen. Ein Beitrag zum Problem der Theologia Naturalis* (Munich: Verlag Schnell und Steiner, 1960).

9. See Encyclical Letter *Deus Caritas Est*, paragraphs 8 (biblical faith purifies the human notion of love) and 28a (how faith purifies practical reason in its attempts to establish justice).

10. These words are virtually verbatim Ratzinger; see *Introduction to Christianity*, p. 100; two pages later he refers to 'the link-up with the God of the philosophers which the Christian faith consciously effected' (the word 'link-up' is a reminder of Augustine's 'dash' or *Bindestrich*).

11. As well as the Bonn inaugural lecture, see, for example, *Introduction to Christianity*, chapters 2 and 3, pp. 88-90, 92-93 and 98-103 especially; see 'Faith, Philosophy and Theology' in *The Nature and Mission of Theology: Essays to Orient Theology in Today's Debates* (San Francisco: Ignatius Press, 1995), pp. 13-29, here pp. 24-27 (this essay is originally from 1984); and see *Deus Caritas Est*, paragraph 9, also 10.

12. *Deus Caritas Est*, paragraph 10.

13. Ratzinger repeatedly speaks in this vein. I catch in it an echo of Hans Urs von Balthasar's essay, 'Who is Man?' There, in answer to the question 'Why am I precisely I?', von Balthasar, on a hint from Saint Thomas, says: 'The

answer can only go: God has meant, willed, loved and chosen *me*'. See 'Who is Man?' in: *Explorations in Theology IV: Spirit and Institution* (San Francisco: Ignatius Press, 1995; original German, 1974), pp. 15-28, here p. 27.

14. See *Introduction to Christianity*, pp. 42-44.

15. I have written a little about this before. See James Corkery, 'Pope Benedict's Theological Approach May Limit his Pastoral Outreach' in: *Irish Times*, Tuesday April 26, 2005, p. 16.

16. See 'Gratia praesupponit naturam. Erwägungen über Sinn und Grenze eines scholastischen Axioms' in *Dogma und Verkündigung* (Munich: Erich Wewel Verlag, 1973): 161-181, here pp. 179-180 (note the indebtedness to Henri de Lubac). Also, see 'Faith as Conversion – Metanoia' in *Principles of Catholic Theology: Building Stones for a Fundamental Theology* (San Francisco: Ignatius Press, 1987), pp. 55-67.

17. See 'Gratia praesupponit naturam', p. 178, also p. 180.

18. See Walter Kasper's response to Joseph Ratzinger's response (!) to K's initial review of *Introduction to Christianity*. This second Kasper text is: 'Theorie und Praxis innerhalb einer theologia crucis: Antwort auf J. Ratzingers 'Glaube, Geschichte und Philosophie' in *Hochland* 62 (March/April 1970): 152-157.

19. See *Introduction to Christianity*, pp. 222-223.

20. See 'Gratia praesupponit naturam', p. 179.

21. See J. Ratzinger's commentary on Part I, chapter 1 of *Gaudium et spes* ('The Dignity of the Human Person') in: Herbert Vorgrimler (ed.), *Commentary on the Documents of Vatican II*. Vol. V (London and New York: Burns & Oates/Herder and Herder), 1969, pp. 115-163, here pp. 159-163.

22. See J. Ratzinger, *The Theology of History in St. Bonaventure*, pp. 117-118; also p. 146.

23. *Ibid.*, see p. 163.

24. See *Introduction to Christianity*, p. 204.

25. Joseph Ratzinger/Benedikt XVI, *Vom Sinn des Christseins: Drei Predigten* (Munich: Kösel, 1965; re-issued 2005), p. 110.

26. *Ibid.*, see pp. 98-99.

27. See *The Theology of History in St Bonaventure*, p. 157.

28. *Ibid.*

29. See Michael A. Fahey, 'Joseph Ratzinger as Ecclesiologist and Pastor', p. 78 and p. 79.

30. See Monika Hellwig, *Understanding Catholicism*. Second Edition (Mahwah, NJ: Paulist Press, 2002), p. 1 and *passim*. Also, see Walter Kasper, *An Introduction to Christian Faith* (London: Burns & Oates and Ramsey, NJ: Paulist Press, 1972, original German 1972), pp. 69-70, also pp. 32-35; and *passim*.

3. On Being Human

1. *Salt of the Earth: The Church at the End of the Millennium.* Interview with Peter Seewald (San Francisco: Ignatius Press, 1997), pp. 55-6.

2. *Ibid.*, see pp. 116-7 and p. 193.

3. See *Introduction to Christianity* (New York: Seabury Press, 1969), p. 12; also *Salt of the Earth*, p. 259.

4. *Die sakramentale Begründung christlicher Existenz* (Meitingen/Freising: Kyrios-Verlag, 1966), p. 19.

5. *Ibid.*, see p. 16; also *Introduction to Christianity*, pp. 273-5; and *Eschatology: Death and Eternal Life* (Washington DC: The Catholic University of America Press, 1988 [original German, 1977]), pp 157-8 (in fact, see sections (c), (d) and (e), pp 150-61).

6. *Eschatology*, see p. 159.

7. *Ibid.*

8. For a recent expression of this idea, see *God and the World* (San Francisco: Ignatius Press, 2002), p. 76.

9. *Ibid.* Also, Cardinal Joseph Ratzinger, *'In the Beginning ... ': A Catholic Understanding of the Story of Creation and the Fall* (Edinburgh: T & T Clark, 1995), p. 45 (original German 1986).

10. See *Eschatology*, p. 155; also *Die sakramentale Begründung*, p. 16, *Introduction to Christianity*, p. 275.

11. See J. Ratzinger, 'Beten in unserer Zeit' in: *Dogma und Verkündigung* (Munich: Wewel, 1973), p. 123.

12. That Ratzinger views the human being first and foremost as a *receiver* has been noted also by David L. Schindler. See his 'Is America Bourgeois?' in *Communio* 14 (Fall 1987): 262-90 (here pp. 267-71).

13. See *Die sakramentale Begründung*, pp. 18-19; see *God and the World*, p. 76.

14. *Salt of the Earth*, p. 41. It is interesting to note that a Christmas card of Pope Benedict in 2005, written in his own hand and copied for many, quoted St Augustine's Sermon 165: '*Expergiscere, homo: quia per te Deus factus est homo*' ('Wake up, human being, because for you God became human').

15. See Ratzinger's *Seek That Which Is Above: Meditations through the Year* (San Francisco: Ignatius Press, 1986), pp. 127-8; also 'Terrorismus, Menschlichkeit und Kirche. Aus Silvesteransprachen an der Jahreswende 1977/78. Kardinal Ratzinger: Die Signatur des Jahres' in: *Herderkorrespondenz* 32 (1978): 84-6 (here 85). Note that, with Augustine, Ratzinger contrasts unbelief/pride with faith/humility, seeing sin, basically, as a problem of 'un-faith', of Godlessness.

16. *Die sakramentale Begründung*, p. 19.

17. *Ibid.*

18. See *Introduction to Christianity*, p. 12.

19. See *Truth and Tolerance: Christian Belief and World Religions* (San Francisco:

Ignatius Press, 2004), p. 79. The original German is *Glaube, Wahrheit, Toleranz. Das Christentum und die Weltreligionen* (Freiburg: Herder, 2003) and above, when I refer to the text, I stay closer to my own translation of this.

20. *Ibid.*, p. 189. Of *truth* Ratzinger says: 'In the beginning, this theme wasn't so central for me' (*Salt of the Earth*, p. 66). It became so, however, as he came 'to grasp that relinquishing truth doesn't solve anything but, on the contrary, leads to the tyranny of caprice ... Man is degraded if he can't know truth, if everything, in the final analysis, is just the product of an individual or collective decision' (*Salt*, p. 67).

21. *Seek That Which Is Above*, p. 32. Also – on the togetherness of freedom and truth – see Ratzinger's 'Freedom and Liberation: The Anthropological Vision of the 1986 Instruction *Libertatis Conscientia*' in: *Church, Ecumenism and Politics: New Essays in Ecclesiology* (New York: Crossroad, 1988), pp. 255-75 (here p. 274). For his ideas on how freedom and truth go together, Ratzinger draws on Romano Guardini, also, and more fundamentally, on Saint Augustine (multiple references available for each!). For a more recent, highly engaging, reflection on this topic, see pp. 231-58 of *Truth and Tolerance*.

22. '*In the Beginning* ... ', p. 71.

23. See *Introduction to Christianity*, p. 223.

24. See J. Ratzinger, *Abbruch und Aufbruch. Die Antwort des Glaubens auf die Krise der Werte* (Munich: Minerva, 1988). This is the published version of a lecture given by Ratzinger in 1987 at the University of Eichstätt in which, drawing on C.S. Lewis's book *The Abolition of Man* (New York: Macmillan, 1947), he showed how Lewis had seen in the loss of 'the doctrine of objective values, which express themselves in the being of the world' (Ratzinger, p. 13) the deadly danger of abolishing the human being (pp. 12-13). (For the German translation used by Ratzinger see *Die Abschaffung des Menschen* [Einsiedeln, 1979]).

25. See *Abbruch und Aufbruch*, pp. 12-16; also *'In the Beginning* ... ', pp. 64-71.

26. *Salt of the Earth*, p. 282.

27. See Joseph Cardinal Ratzinger with Vittorio Messori, *The Ratzinger Report: An Exclusive Interview on the State of the Church* (San Francisco: Ignatius Press, 1985), p. 81.

28. See *Introduction to Christianity*, pp. 133-7, also 155-6 and 175-82; also 'Retrieving the Tradition: Concerning the Notion of Person in Theology' in: *Communio* 17 (Fall 1990): 439-54 (here 445-50).

29. *Ibid.* Also *'In the Beginning* ... ', pp. 57-8, and 48-9; and *Introduction to Christianity*, pp. 222-3.

30. See *Introduction to Christianity*, p. 211; also Ratzinger's *The Open Circle: The Meaning of Christian Brotherhood* (New York: Sheed & Ward, 1966, original German 1960), p. 60.

31. See *Introduction to Christianity*, pp. 175-6.

32. See Ratzinger's *The God of Jesus Christ* (Chicago, Illinois: Franciscan Herald Press, 1979), p. 47.

33. See 'Salvation History, Metaphysics and Eschatology' in Ratzinger's *Principles of Catholic Theology: Building Stones for a Fundamental Theology* (San Francisco: Ignatius Press, 1987), pp. 171-90, at 187.

34. See *'In the Beginning ...* ', p. 48.

35. *Ibid.*, see pp. 48-9.

36. *Ibid.*, see p. 49.

37. *Ibid.* Recall that this centrality of the *mysterium paschale* was highlighted also in my last article.

38. *Ibid.*, p. 58.

39. See a key essay, 'Faith as Conversion – Metanoia' in *Principles of Catholic Theology*, pp. 55-67.

40. See 'Why I am Still in the Church' in: Hans Urs von Balthasar and Joseph Ratzinger, *Two Say Why* (London and Chicago: Search Press Ltd. and Franciscan Herald Press, 1973), pp. 66-90, here p. 70.

41. Francis Schüssler Fiorenza, 'From Theologian to Pope: A personal view back, past the public portrayals,' in: *Harvard Divinity Bulletin* (Autumn 2005): 56-62 (here p. 61).

42. See *'Gratia praesupponit naturam.* Erwägungen über Sinn und Grenze eines scholastischen Axioms', in: *Dogma und Verkündigung*, pp. 161-81 (here p. 161). And see Söhngen's 'Analogie fidei' I and II in: *Catholica* 3 (1934): 113-36 and 176-208; and *Die Einheit in der Theologie* (Munich, 1952), pp. 235-64.

43. See *'Gratia praesupponit naturam,'* p. 161.

44. *Ibid.*

45. However, I detect a growth in appreciation of Aquinas (specifically regarding the relationship between the natural and the supernatural) over the years. E.g., see *'In the Beginning ...* ', pp. 79-80 and pp. 94-5.

46. *'Gratia praesupponit naturam'*, p. 178.

47. Joseph Cardinal Ratzinger, *Called to Communion: Understanding the Church Today* (San Francisco: Ignatius Press, 1996; original German 1991), p. 148.

48. See *'In the Beginning ...* ', pp. 61-4.

49. See 'Der Wortgebrauch von *natura* und die beginnende Verselbständigung der Metaphysik bei Bonaventura' in: P. Wilpert (ed.), *Die Metaphysik im Mittelalter* (= Miscellanea Mediaevalia vol. 2), published in Berlin in 1963.

50. On how all nature, all of creation, is ultimately grace for Bonaventure, see 'Der Wortgebrauch von *natura,'* p. 495, and *'Gratia praesupponit naturam,'* p. 173. In both texts, Bonaventure's words *hoc totum quod fecit fuit gratia* are cited (see Bonaventure's *I Sent.*, d. 44, a. 1, q. 1, ad 4 [I 784b]).

51. E. Gilson, *The Unity of Philosophical Experience* (New York: Charles Scribner's Sons, 1948), p. 52.

52. *Ibid.*

53. See, for example, *The Breviloquium* in: *The Works of Bonaventure: Cardinal,*

Seraphic Doctor and Saint, vol. II (Paterson, NJ: St. Anthony Guild Press, 1963), Part V, chapter 2, paragraph 3; also Part III, chapter 1, paragraph 3.

54. Avery Dulles, 'The Extraordinary Synod of 1985' in: *The Reshaping of Catholicism: Current Challenges in the Theology of Church* (San Francisco: Harper & Row, 1988), pp. 184-206 (here p. 191).

55. *Ibid.*

56. *Ibid.* The second school named by Dulles and, for space reasons, not to be investigated here, exhibited rather opposing characteristics to the first. It still welcomed an openness of the Church to the world. The words used by Dulles to characterise it were 'communitarian' and 'humanistic' (p. 192).

57. See *Volk und Haus Gottes in Augustins Lehre von der Kirche* (Munich: Karl Zink Verlag, 1954), pp. 8-11, 14, 23-7, 151-2 and 226.

58. *Ibid.*, see p. 8-11, 26-7, 151-2 and 218-34.

59. *Ibid.*, see pp. 226-8.

60. Commentary on Introductory Article and Chapter One of *Gaudium et spes* in: Herbert Vorgrimler (ed.), *Commentary on the Documents of Vatican II*, V (New York: Herder & Herder, 1969), pp 115-63, at 155.

61. See J. Ratzinger, 'Salvation and History' in: *Principles of Catholic Theology*, pp. 153-71 (here 166). The text of Rahner that he is contesting is in *Grundkurs des Glaubens* (Freiburg: Herder, 1976), p. 388. The English version is in *Foundations of Christian Faith* (New York: The Seabury Press, 1978), p. 402.

62. See 'Salvation and History,' p. 166.

63. Inclusive language failure here is due to the German *Mensch* (inclusive) becoming 'man' in English.

64. See John Henry Newman, 'Remembrance of Past Mercies' in: *Parochial and Plain Sermons* (San Francisco: Ignatius Press, 1987), pp. 997-1005 (here p. 1004). I am indebted to my confrère, Daniel Patrick Huang, S.J., for first drawing my attention to this delightful text of Newman.

4. Understanding Salvation

1. Joseph Ratzinger, 'Vorfragen zu einer Theologie der Erlösung,' in: Leo Scheffczyk (ed.), *Erlösung und Emanzipation*. Quaestiones Disputatae 61 (Freiburg-im-Breisgau: Herder, 1973), pp. 141-155, at p. 141.

2. See Ratzinger's essay, 'Die Zukunft des Heils,' in: Ulrich Hommes and Joseph Ratzinger, *Das Heil des Menschen. Innerweltlich-Christlich* (Munich: Kösel Verlag, 1975), pp. 31-63, at pp. 35-37. There is no specific mention of Metz in these pages, but Ratzinger clearly has him in mind as he bemoans a range of theological developments that have been taking place; see, for example, the reference on p. 36 to [Metz's] notion of 'dangerous memory'.

3. See Ratzinger's *Politik und Erlösung. Zum Verhältnis von Glaube, Rationalität und Irrationalem in der sogenannten Theologie der Befreiung* (hereafter

Politik und Erlösung). Rheinisch-Westfälische Akademie der Wissenschaften, Vorträge G 279 (Opladen: Westdeutscher Verlag GmbH, 1986), pp. 15-20. See also his essay, 'Freedom and Liberation: The Anthropological Vision of the 1986 Instruction *Libertatis Conscientia*' in: Joseph Cardinal Ratzinger, *Church, Ecumenism and Politics* (New York: Crossroad, 1988), pp. 255-275, at pp. 271-274.

4. See Ratzinger's essay, 'Der Christ und die Welt von heute. Überlegungen zur Pastoralkonstitution des Zweiten Vatikanischen Konzils,' in: J. Ratzinger, *Dogma und Verkündigung* (Munich: Erich Wewel Verlag, 1973), pp. 183-204, at 195-200. See also my unpublished dissertation, *The Relationship between Human Existence and Christian Salvation in the Theology of Joseph Ratzinger* (Washington DC: The Catholic University of America, 1991), p. 24. (This dissertation – hereafter *Dissertation* – is also available from University Microfilms International, Ann Arbor, Michigan, order # 9203408, copyright James Corkery). On the notion of 'makeability' (*Machbarkeit*), the chief influence on Ratzinger is Hans Freyer, *Theorie des gegenwärtigen Zeitalters* (Stuttgart, 1958), pp. 15-31 especially.

5. See J. Ratzinger, 'Heil: II. Theologisch' in: *Lexikon für Theologie und Kirche* V (1960), pp. 78-80, at p. 78. And *Dissertation*, p. 13.

6. See 'Heil: II. Theologisch,' p. 78, and *Dissertation*, p. 13.

7. See 'Heil: II. Theologisch,' p. 78, and *Dissertation*, pp. 13-14.

8. See 'Die Zukunft des Heils,' p. 33; also Ratzinger's *Eschatology: Death and Eternal Life* (Washington DC: The Catholic University of America Press, 1988, Second English edition 2007), pp. 13-15; and *Dissertation*, p. 14.

9. See 'Die Zukunft des Heils,' pp. 33-41, and *Dissertation*, pp. 15-20.

10. See *Dissertation*, p. 15, and Ratzinger's book, *Behold the Pierced One: An Approach to a Spiritual Christology* (San Francisco: Ignatius Press, 1986, original German 1984), p. 14.

11. Notice how Pope Benedict, in his Encyclical letter, *Spe Salvi* (nn. 13-15), also opposes this individualism, drawing (see n.13) on Henri de Lubac's famous book *Catholicisme: Aspects sociaux du dogme* (1983, original text 1937). For the encyclical in English translation, see *Spe Salvi* (Rome: Libreria Editrice Vaticana, 2007).

12. Note the Marxist echo in 'full equality of everyone' (and see *Spe Salvi*, nn. 20 and 21).

13. See *Dissertation*, pp. 15-17, and accompanying footnotes, noting especially 'Die Zukunft des Heils,' pp. 33-41.

14. See 'Die Zukunft des Heils,' p. 34, and *Eschatology: Death and Eternal Life*, p. 14; *Dissertation*, p. 17.

15. *Dissertation*, p. 18 (and 'Die Zukunft des Heils,' p. 35).

16. *Dissertation*, see p. 18; and see 'Die Zukunft des Heils,' p. 33.

17. See 'Vorfragen zu einer Theologie der Erlösung,' pp. 146-147 and pp. 154-155.

18. *Ibid.*

19. *Ibid.*, see p. 154, also p. 147. See Congregation for the Doctrine of the Faith, Instruction on *Christian Freedom and Liberation* (United States Catholic Conference, 1986), paragraph 75; and see *Spe Salvi*, nn. 24 (a) and (b) and 25.

20. See 'Vorfragen zu einer Theologie der Erlösung,' p. 147; *Politik und Erlösung,* p. 23; 'Freedom and Liberation,' pp. 271-272; 'Church and Economy: Responsibility for the Future of the World Economy,' in: *Communio* 13 (Fall 1986), pp. 199-204 (especially 204); and *Spe Salvi*, n. 25.

21. See 'Die Zukunft des Heils,' p. 42; also 'Vorfragen zu einer Theologie der Erlösung,' p. 143.

22. Hence the procedure followed in this chapter, where I move from Ratzinger's robust views on what salvation is not to his consideration of what 'the faith' says about salvation. Notice that this procedure is evident in Ratzinger's (Pope Benedict's) own encyclical *Spe Salvi*, in which nn. 16-23 highlight the mistakes of the modern age regarding Christian hope and nn. 24-31 deal with 'The True Shape of Christian Hope'.

23. See Ferdinand Schumacher, 'Ich glaube an die Auferstehung der Toten. Das Ende der Zeit in der Theologie Joseph Ratzingers' in: Frank Meier-Hamidi and Ferdinand Schumacher (editors), *Der Theologe Joseph Ratzinger.* Quaestiones Disputatae 222 (Freiburg-im-Breisgau: Verlag Herder, 2007), pp. 73-99, at pp. 76 and pp. 81-83.

24. See Erwin Discherl, 'Gott und Mensch als Beziehungswesen. Die theologische und anthropologische Denkfigur Joseph Ratzingers ausgehend von der Christologie' in: *Der Theologe Joseph Ratzinger,* pp. 56-72, at p. 65.

25. See 'Die Zukunft des Heils,' p. 42.

26. See *Dissertation,* p. 21, drawing on Ratzinger's 'Faith and Knowledge' in: *Faith and the Future* (Chicago: Franciscan Herald Press, 1971), pp. 3-24, at pp. 23-24 and also Ratzinger's essay 'What Constitutes Christian Faith Today?' in: *Principles of Catholic Theology: Building Stones for a Fundamental Theology* (San Francisco: Ignatius Press, 1987), pp. 15-27, at p. 26.

27. See 'Heil: II. Theologisch,' p. 79.

28. See 'Mittler: II. Dogmatisch,' in: *Lexikon für Theologie und Kirche* VII (1962): 499-502, at 501.

29. See 'Sühne: V. Systematisch,' in: *Lexikon für Theologie und Kirche* IX (1964): 1156-1158, at 1158.

30. See 'Stellvertretung,' in: Heinrich Fries (ed.), *Handbuch Theologischer Grundbegriffe* II (Munich, 1963): 566-575, at 574.

31. See 'Christ is the Apex of the History of Salvation,' General Audience of Pope Benedict XVI on the figure of St. Paul on Wednesday November 8, 2006; text accessed at www.ewtn.com/vnews/getstory.asp?number =73145.

32. Pope Benedict in Cologne, 18 August 2005, echoing his own inauguration homily of April 24, 2005. See *God's Revolution: World Youth Day and*

other Cologne Talks (San Francisco: Ignatius Press, 2006), p. 39.

33. *Ibid.*, see pp. 35 and 36.

34. See 'Vorfragen zu einer Theologie der Erlösung,' p. 152.

35. Here there is an interesting twist. We have shown already how Ratzinger repeatedly rejects the idea that we can be saved by what comes 'from outside' when what is meant by this are human creations/arrangements that act upon us without involving our freedom and participation. Jesus Christ, the help sent 'from outside' (but not created by us) does not do his work by bypassing our freedom, but enters into its very depths, inviting our participation, enlisting our involvement, opening our hearts. He is help from outside that transforms us inside.

36. See 'Vorfragen zu einer Theologie der Erlösung,' pp. 152-153, also pp. 145 and 149.

37. *Ibid.*, see p. 148; and note that Ratzinger's ideas here rely on Joseph Pieper's book, *Über die Liebe* (Munich, 1972), pp. 38-105 especially.

38. *Ibid.*, p. 149.

39. *Ibid.*, p. 143; see also Ratzinger's *Introduction to Christianity* (New York: The Seabury Press, 1969), p. 202.

40. *Ibid.*, the entire article.

41. *Ibid.*, see p. 147 (indeed pp. 145-147).

42. 'Vorfragen zu einer Theologie der Erlösung,' p. 153 (this passage is a challenge to translate inclusively).

43. See *Dissertation*, pp. 42-77 and pp. 81-144 for a teasing out of these gifts and their effects in Christians' lives.

44. See Ratzinger's essay, 'Salvation History, Metaphysics and Eschatology,' in: *Principles of Catholic Theology*, pp. 171-190, at pp. 187-188. See also *Dissertation*, pp. 53-54 and p. 25, note 26.

45. *Ibid.*, see pp. 186-188.

46. *Ibid.*, p. 187.

47. *Ibid.*, p. 188.

48. 'Heil: II. Theologisch,' p. 79; see also p. 80: 'Mit Christus ist also bereits echte Heilsgegenwart gesetzt.'

49. Space does not permit listing multiple mentions here, but see *Dissertation*, p. 42, note 62.

50. See Ratzinger's essay, 'Faith as Conversion – Metanoia,' in *Principles of Catholic Theology*, pp. 55-67, at p. 60.

51. See Ratzinger's 'Baptism, Faith and Membership in the Church – the Unity of Structure and Content,' in *Principles of Catholic Theology*, pp. 27-43, at pp. 31-33; also, see *Dissertation*, pp. 88-99.

52. *Ibid.*, see p. 33.

53. *Ibid.* And see *Dissertation*, p. 98, note 33, pointing out the influence of both de Lubac and von Balthasar.

54. See 'Faith as Conversion – Metanoia,' p. 65; and see *Dissertation*,

pp. 94-95.

55. See 'Baptism, Faith and Membership in the Church,' pp. 32-33, and *Dissertation*, pp. 91-92.

56. Note the Augustinian themes in this portrayal of sin; recall also chapter 3; and see *Dissertation*, pp. 81-100.

57. I tease this out in detail in *Dissertation*, pp. 102-129 (on participation in Jesus' 'for-existence,' see pp. 109f.).

58. See *The God of Jesus Christ: Meditations on God in the Trinity* (Chicago: Franciscan Herald Press, 1979), p. 61.

59. See Ratzinger's early book, *The Open Circle: The Meaning of Christian Brotherhood* (New York: Sheed and Ward, 1966, original German 1960), p. 101. See also his dissertation, *Volk und Haus Gottes in Augustins Lehre von der Kirche* (Munich: Karl Zink Verlag, 1954), pp. 197-218 especially. Finally, see *Dissertation*, p. 102, note 38.

60. See *Dissertation*, p. 145.

61. This notion of Christ the representative (*Stellvertreter*) and of Christians participating in his service (*Dienst*) of representing humanity before God, of 'standing in' for us, is prominent also in Ratzinger's soteriology, deserving much more attention than I can give it here. See 'Stellvertretung,' p. 574 (indeed pp. 573-575); see *Introduction to Christianity*, pp. 217-219, especially 219; also pp. 187-189. And see Ratzinger's essay 'Kein Heil ausserhalb der Kirche?,' in: *Das neue Volk Gottes. Entwürfe zur Ekklesiologie* (Düsseldorf: Patmos Verlag,1969), pp. 339-361, especially pp. 357f.

62. See 'Kein Heil ausserhalb der Kirche?,' pp. 358-359.

63. See 'On Hans Küng's *Being a Christian*' in: *Doctrine & Life* 27: 5 (1977): 3-17, at p. 17. See also Hans Küng, *On Being a Christian* (New York: Doubleday, 1976), pp. 440-444: 'Deification or Humanization?'

64. 'Die Zukunft des Heils,' p. 44.

65. *Ibid.*, see pp. 43-50. These three key points concerning resurrection faith are discussed in many other places in Ratzinger's writings also, especially in his book *Eschatology: Death and Eternal Life*, where many controversial matters are taken up (see, at least, pp. 112-140, 165-194 and 213-214). See also 'Salvation History, Metaphysics and Eschatology,' pp. 181-184 especially. On p. 184, Ratzinger points to the utter centrality, for Christian faith, of the statement *Jesus ist auferstanden* (= the original German words – see *Theologische Prinzipienlehre*, p. 193). I would translate these words as 'Jesus *is* risen' even though the translator chooses 'Jesus *has* risen' because in this essay Ratzinger tries not to lose sight of the ontological – one could say the *is* – aspect of the faith that is expressed already in Christian belief in Jesus' resurrection (even while he seeks to remain true also to a salvation-historical perspective). On this, see also p. 190; and see *Dissertation*, pp. 72-73.

66. See *Eschatology: Death and Eternal Life*, chapter V (and its history of reception – a worthwhile object of study).

67. See *Introduction to Christianity*, pp. 202-203, also p. 278. See Ratzinger's Commentary on the Introductory article and Chapter One of *Gaudium et spes* in: Herbert Vorgrimler (ed.), *Commentary on the Documents of Vatican II*, Vol. V (New York: Herder & Herder, 1969), pp. 115-163, at p. 156. (See also *Spe Salvi*, n. 28).

68. Joseph Ratzinger, *Seek That Which is Above: Meditations through the Year.* Second Edition (San Francisco: Ignatius Press, 2007), p. 72.

69 This is Martin Luther's position, robustly stated in his lectures on Galatians. See 'Lectures on Galatians 1535, Chapters 1-4,' in: *Luther's Works* Vol. 26. Editor Jaroslav Pelikan and Associate Editor Walter A. Hansen. USA: St. Louis, MO: Concordia Publishing House, 1963, pp. 133 and 137-138.

70. Recall 'Vorfragen zu einer Theologie der Erlösung,' pp. 151-155.

71. See M. Luther, 'Lectures on Galatians' (here 2:16), pp. 133-138; and *Dissertation*, pp. 211-212 and 162-167.

72. See *Politik und Erlösung*, pp. 15-20, especially p. 18.

73 See: *The Ratzinger Report*, pp. 79 and 172-173; 'Heil II,' p. 79; and 'Faith as Conversion – Metanoia,' p. 60.

74. Ratzinger's mistrust of human activity is reminiscent of Augustine's. On the latter's, see Frederick H. Russell, "Only Something Good Can be Evil': The Genesis of Augustine's Secular Ambivalence' in: *Theological Studies* 51:4 (December 1990): 698-716, at 709, where the author refers to 'Augustine's profound ambivalence regarding the motives and results of human activity' (Russell finds this ambivalence in the later Augustine particularly.)

75. See 'Vorfragen zu einer Theologie der Erlösung,' p. 153.

76. See the 1986 CDF Instruction *Libertatis Conscientia*, n. 74, and *Spe Salvi*, n. 25.

77. This approach was referred to already; note 20 above highlights several allusions to it in Ratzinger's works.

78. For the English text, see Austin Flannery, O.P. (General Editor), *Vatican II: Constitutions, Decreees, Declaration* (Dublin: Dominican Publications, 1996), p. 205; the significant words in the original Latin are: '*Regni Dei magnopere interest.*' For a more detailed treatment, see my (forthcoming) article 'Joseph Ratzinger on Liberation Theology: What Did He Say? Why Did He Say It? What Can Be Said About It?' Proceedings of the Conference on Liberation Theology held from October 3-4, 2008, at the Milltown Institute of Theology and Philosophy, Dublin (section of the talk entitled 'Earthly Progress and the Growth of the Kingdom'), to be published later in 2009 by Peter Lang.

79. See again *Gaudium et spes*, n. 39; and see Congregation for the Doctrine of the Faith Instruction *Libertatis Conscientia*, n. 60.

80. See Gustavo Gutiérrez, *A Theology of Liberation: History, Politics and Salvation* (Maryknoll, NY: Orbis Books, 1973), pp. 168-171 and p. 177.

81. *Ibid.*, see p. 177.

82. See again 'Vorfragen zu einer Theologie der Erlösung,' pp. 145 and 153.

5. *Quaestiones Disputatae:*
Walter Kasper and Gustavo Gutiérrez

1. 'Das Wesen des Christlichen. B' in: *Theologische Revue* 3 (Jahrgang 65:1969): 182-188.

2. 'Glaube, Geschichte und Philosophie. Zum Echo auf *Einführung in das Christentum*', in: *Hochland* 61 (1969: November/Dezember): 533-543.

3. 'Theorie und Praxis innerhalb einer *theologia crucis*: Antwort auf Joseph Ratzingers Glaube, Geschichte und Philosophie. Zum Echo auf *Einführung in das Christentum*', in: *Hochland* 62 (1970: März/April): 152-157.

4. *Ibid.*, 'Schlusswort', pp. 157-159.

5. See 'Das Wesen des Christlichen. B', pp 184 and185; also 'Theorie und Praxis', p. 155.

6. See 'Das Wesen des Christlichen. B,' p. 184.

7. *Ibid.*, see pp. 185-186.

8. *Introduction to Christianity* (New York: The Seabury Press, 1969; original German 1968), p. 25.

9. See 'Das Wesen des Christlichen. B,' p. 187; also, 'Theorie und Praxis,' p. 155.

10. *Ibid.*, see p. 185; also 'Theorie und Praxis', p. 152.

11. *Ibid.*, see p. 184.

12. *Introduction to Christianity*, p. 203 (commented on in 'Das Wesen des Christlichen. B,' p. 184).

13. See 'Das Wesen des Christilichen. B,' p. 184 (also p. 185).

14. *Ibid.*, p. 185.

15. 'Glaube, Geschichte und Philosophie,' p. 536.

16. *Ibid.*, p. 537.

17. *Ibid.*.

18. *Ibid.*, quoting Kasper's 'Das Wesen des Christlichen. B,' p. 186.

19. W. Kasper, 'Theorie und Praxis,' p. 155, footnote 14.

20. *Ibid.*, see pp. 152-153.

21. *Ibid.*, see pp. 155 and 152.

22. See Ratzinger, 'Schlusswort,' p. 157.

23. *Ibid.*, p. 158.

24. See 'Glaube, Geschichte und Philosophie,' p. 537; also see 'Theorie und Praxis,' p. 155 and note 14.

25. Walter Kasper, 'On the Church,' in: *The Tablet* (23 June 2001): 927-930, at 930. For reasons of space I cannot go into this more recent dispute here, details of which are available, in any case, in several other places. I mention just two: Kilian McDonnell O.S.B., 'The Ratzinger/ Kasper Debate: The Universal Church and Local Churches,' in: *Theological Studies* 63:2 (June 2002): 227-250; and William A. Clark, S.J., *A Voice of Their Own: The Authority of the Local Parish* (Collegeville, MN: The Liturgical Press, 2005), chapter 5:

'Local Authority and the 'Priority of the Universal',' pp. 133-162.

26. A qualified Platonism is evident in his work. Recall his own remark (limited by its context, of course) in *Salt of the Earth* (San Francisco: Ignatius Press, 1997, p.41): 'To a certain extent I am a Platonist.' Also, his roots in Augustine make his Platonism unsurprising: see Aidan Nichols, *The Theology of Joseph Ratzinger* (Edinburgh: T & T Clark, 1988, p. 169). Further, Avery Dulles remarked – admittedly when *denying* Plato's influence on Ratzinger's position regarding the relationship between the universal and particular Churches – 'I suspect that Ratzinger has a certain affinity for Christian Platonism' ('A Zenit Daily Dispatch,' 28 May 2001, found at: www.ewtn.com/library/Theology/ZRTZKSP.HTM, 15/11/'05).

27. J. Ratzinger, *Faith and the Future* (Chicago: Franciscan Herald Press, 1970), pp. 81-83.

28. See 'Vorfragen zu einer Theologie der Erlösung,' in: Leo Scheffczyk (ed.), *Erlösung und Emanzipation.* Quaestiones Disputatae 61 (Freiburg-im-Breisgau, Herder, 1973), pp. 141-155; and 'Die Zukunft des Heils,' in: Ulrich Hommes and Joseph Ratzinger, *Das Heil des Menschen – Innerweltlich, Christlich* (Munich: Kösel Verlag, 1975), pp. 31-63.

29. 'Freedom and Liberation: The Anthropological Vision of the 1986 Instruction *Libertatis Conscientia*', in: J. Ratzinger, *Church, Ecumenism and Politics* (New York: Crossroad, 1988), pp. 255-275.

30. *Politik und Erlösung. Zum Verhältnis von Glaube, Rationalität und Irrationalem in der sogenannten Theologie der Befreiung.* Rheinisch-Westfälische Akademie der Wissenschaften, Vorträge G 279 (Opladen: Westdeutscher Verlag GmbH, 1986).

31. *Ibid.*, see pp. 15-17.

32. *Ibid*, see pp. 18-19; also p. 20. See also Michael Sievernich S.J., 'Von der Utopie zur Ethik. Zur Theologie von Gustavo Gutierrez,' in: *Theologie und Philophie* (1996): 33-46, at 43, where Sievernich casts doubt not on Ratzinger's analysis but on his attribution of Gutierrez's views to Saint-Simon's influence. This doubt does not appear to be shared by Christian Schäfer. See his 'Politik und Erlösung im Spiegel der zwei *civitates*' in: *Münchener Theologische Zeitschrift* 56 (Sonderheft 5/2005): 415-434.

33. *A Theology of Liberation.* Fifteenth anniversary edition (Maryknoll, NY: Orbis Books, 1988), p. xviii.

34. *Ibid.*, p. xix; here see pp. xviii-xix.

35. *Ibid.*, p. xviii.

36. *Ibid.*, p. xxi.

37. *Ibid.*, see p. xviii, also p. xxxviii.

38. *Ibid.*, see p. xxxviii.

39. *Ibid.*

40. *Ibid.*, p. xxxix.

41. See M. Sievernich, 'Von der Utopie zur Ethik,' p. 44.

42. *Ibid.*, see p. 39.

43. *A Theology of Liberation* (1988), p. xl.

44. *Ibid.*, see p. xxxii.

45. *Ibid.*, see pp. xxxiii-xxxiv.

46. *Ibid.*, p. xxxiv.

47. See Dennis M. Doyle, 'Utopia and Utopianism,' in: *New Catholic Encyclopedia*, vol. 18 (Washington DC: The Catholic University of America, 1989): 527-9.

48. See Dennis M. Doyle, *Communion Ecclesiology: Vision and Versions* (Maryknoll, NY: Orbis Books, 2000), p. 117. The text of Karl Mannheim being referred to here is *Ideology and Utopia* (London, 1936).

6. *Quaestiones Disputatae:* Theological Dissent

1. See 'The Church's Teaching Authority – Faith – Morals,' in: Heinz Schürmann, Joseph Ratzinger and Hans Urs von Balthasar, *Principles of Christian Morality* (San Francisco: Ignatius Press, 1986; original German 1975), pp. 45-73, here p. 72 and pp. 47-49. See also 'The Future of the World Through the Hope of Men,' in: *Faith and the Future* (Chicago: Franciscan Herald Press, 1971), pp. 77-88, here pp. 82-83.

2. See Richard A. McCormick, *The Critical Calling: Reflections on Moral Dilemmas since Vatican II* (Washington DC: Georgetown University Press, 1989), p. 90.

3. *The Ratzinger Report: An Exclusive Interview on the State of the Church* (San Francisco: Ignatius Press, 1985).

4. David Gibson, *The Rule of Benedict: Pope Benedict XVI and his Battle with the Modern World* (USA: HarperSanFrancisco, 2006), p. 370, n. 13.

5. Quoted in McCormick, *The Critical Calling*, p. 90 (and see *National Catholic Reporter*, September 6, 1985).

6. See *The Critical Calling*, p. 90.

7. Nicholas Lash, 'II: Catholic Theology and the Crisis of Classicism,' in 'Ratzinger on the Faith: A Response,' Special Issue of *New Blackfriars* 66:780 (June 1985): 279-287, at 283; also 281.

8. Eamon Duffy, 'I: Urbi, but not Orbi ... the Cardinal, the Church, and the World,' in: *New Blackfriars* (June 1985): 272-278, at 273 and 275 (the words in double quotation marks are quotations from Ratzinger in Duffy's text).

9. See McCormick, *The Critical Calling*, pp 6-8, pp 90-91, and *passim*. Also, see Charles E. Curran, *Loyal Dissent: Memoir of a Catholic Theologian* (Washington DC: Georgetown University Press, 2006), chapter 5 ('Investigation and Condemnation'), pp. 107-135.

10. Much ink has been spilled on the distinction between infallible and

non-infallible magisterial teachings. Clearly there is no question of Catholics dissenting from the former. Nor are the latter – for example, documents of the papal magisterium, or of bishops teaching authoritatively in their own dioceses – to be treated as if they are not authoritative and can be approached without an attitude of sincere openness to their truth. However they cannot demand the same kind of unconditional assent as infallible teachings. In moral matters in particular – conscience having been attentively and diligently formed – it can still be the case that dissent from this or that teaching will occur. This is in no way to disparage the Church's guidance in such matters – or indeed in any matter. However, it does acknowledge that, even with the help of the Holy Spirit, the fallible human element in teachings of the ordinary magisterium can mean that they are not free from error. For a much fuller discussion, see the articles 'Magisterium' and 'Dissent' in: Christopher O'Donnell, O.Carm., *Ecclesia: A Theological Encyclopedia of the Church* (Collegeville, MN: The Liturgical Press, 1996), pp. 281-285 and pp. 134-136 respectively.

11. See especially pp. 19-26 (on the CDF and its service) and pp. 83-91 (on 'The Drama of Morality').

12. Published, in a fresh translation from the German, in 1995, under the title 'The Spiritual Basis and Ecclesial Identity of Theology' in: Joseph Cardinal Ratzinger, *The Nature and Mission of Theology: Approaches to Understanding its Role in the Light of Present Controversy* (San Francisco: Ignatius Press, 1995), pp. 45-72.

13. See Congregation for the Doctrine of the Faith, *Instruction on the Ecclesial Vocation of the Theologian* (Rome, May 24, 1990), accessed November 16, 2006, on the Vatican website (www.vatican.va).

14. See 'On the "Instruction concerning the Ecclesial Vocation of the Theologian",' in: *The Nature and Mission of Theology*, pp. 101-120.

15. See *The Ratzinger Report*, pp. 24 and 26; also *Instruction on the Ecclesial Vocation of the Theologian*, number 37 (also 34).

16. *The Ratzinger Report*, p. 24.

17. *Ibid.*, see p. 26.

18. See *Instruction on the Ecclesial Vocation of the Theologian*, paragraph 34. And see Francis A. Sullivan, S.J., 'The Theologian's Ecclesial Vocation and the 1990 CDF Instruction,' in: *Theological Studies* 52 (1991): 51-68 (here p. 67).

19. 'The Spiritual Basis and Ecclesial Identity of Theology,' p. 63. See also *The Ratzinger Report*, p. 25.

20. See *The Ratzinger Report*, p. 24; also p. 26. And see the *Instruction on the Ecclesial Vocation of the Theologian*, nn. 34 and 37.

21. See (at the very least) *The Ratzinger Report*, pp. 19-20, 24-26, 86-91 and 188-190.

22. *Ibid.*, p. 87.

23. *Ibid.*, see pp. 86-88; also p. 20. See also McCormick, *The Critical Calling*, p. 8 and John Mahoney SJ, 'III: On the Other Hand…' in: *New Black-*

friars (June 1985): 288-298, at 293-294. See also Charles E. Curran, *Loyal Dissent*, pp. 115-116 (noting, in particular, the unnuanced 1984 quotation from Ratzinger).

24. See *The Ratzinger Report* again, p. 87.

25. *Ibid.*, see pp. 186-187; also p. 175; and p. 20.

26. *Ibid.*, see p. 25; and see 'The Spiritual Basis and Ecclesial Identity of Theology,' p. 69.

27. See McCormick, *The Critical Calling*, p. 93, note 14; also pp. 81-82, and p. 113. In all of these places, Ratzinger's 'typical Catholics' are unmasked as being much more likely to be Catholics of the far right. On p. 81, a remark of John Tracy Ellis, at that time probably the leading U.S. Church historian, is quoted: 'I have the impression that certain curia officials are listening too much to one side – and that side is usually the far right.'

28. *The Ratzinger Report*, p. 26. See also 'On the 'Instruction concerning the Ecclesial Vocation of the Theologian',' p. 117, where Ratzinger refers to theologians reproaching the magisterium with mistrust and wonders where they detect it. In the remark quoted above, they detect it in the Prefect of the CDF!

29. See McCormick, *The Critical Calling*, p. 19 (McCormick is drawing on Yves Congar, also Avery Dulles). See also p. 83 and p. 167.

30. *Ibid.*, see p. 19 (italics mine).

31. Francis A. Sullivan, 'The Theologian's Ecclesial Vocation and the 1990 CDF Instruction,' p. 60.

32. *Ibid.*

33. See 'On the "Instruction concerning the Ecclesial Vocation of the Theologian",' p. 117, and 'Zur "Instruktion über die kirchliche Berufung des Theologen",' in: Joseph Kardinal Ratzinger, *Wesen und Auftrag der Theologie* (Freiburg: Johannes Verlag, 1993), pp. 89-107, at p. 104.

34. See *The Ecclesial Vocation of the Theologian*, nn. 25-31 and nn. 32-40; see 'On the "Instruction concerning the Ecclesial Vocation of the Theologian",' pp. 116-117.

35. See n. 32.

36. Francis Sullivan, S.J., 'The Theologian's Ecclesial Vocation and the 1990 CDF Instruction,' p. 68.

37. See R. McCormick, *The Critical Calling*, pp. 76-77.

38. Names that come to mind – this list is by no means exhaustive – are: Leonardo Boff, Charles Curran, Edward Schillebeeckx, Gustavo Gutiérrez, Matthew Fox, Marciano Vidal, Ivone Gabarra, Anthony De Mello, Reinhard Messner, Jeannine Gramick and Robert Nugent, Eugen Drewermann, Tissa Balasuriya, Lavinia Byrne, Jacques Dupuis and Roger Haight. (The cases of Hans Küng, Jacques Pohier and others were already in the 'pipeline' under Ratzinger's predecessor, Cardinal Franjo Seper).

39. Charles Curran, *Loyal Dissent*, pp. 126-132 ('My Response to the

Vatican Condemnation') and p. 121.

40. F. Sullivan, 'The Theologian's Ecclesial Vocation and the 1990 CDF Instruction,' p. 66.

41. See 'The Spiritual Basis and Ecclesial Identity of Theology,' pp. 48-50.

42. *Ibid.*. A read of the entire essay will confirm this impression.

43. See Joseph Cardinal Ratzinger, 'Letters: Church, Pope and Gospel,' in: *The Tablet*, 26 October 1991, pp. 130-131, at p. 131.

44. See *The Ratzinger Report*, p. 25.

45. *Instruction on the Ecclesial Vocation of the Theologian*, n. 37 (italics mine). Following the quoted words is a footnote to the Apostolic Constitution of John Paul II, *Sapientia Christiana*, n. 27, 1 and also a footnote to canon 812 of the Code of Canon Law, which reads: 'Those who teach theological subjects in any institute of higher studies must have a mandate from the competent ecclesiastical authority.'

46. Recall Curran's remarks referred to earlier. The other theologians mentioned above have written also, as most readers will be well aware, of their difficult experiences interacting with the CDF.

47. See Eamon Duffy, 'Urbi, but not Orbi...,' p. 277: Countering what he sees as Ratzinger's 'simple church/world dualism,' Duffy writes concerning the Church: 'All its thinking, and even more obviously, all its institutions, draw on and are conditioned by "worldly" models, and are thereby implicated in the relativism and imperfection of the created order.' Basically I agree. Ratzinger tends to an idealization, a spiritualization, of the Church; however, Church and world, while distinct, are never concretely separate.

48. Here see nn. 28-31 in particular.

49. See the Pope's message for World Food Day 2006, 'Feeding the Hungry and Removing the Obstacles to Make it Happen,' in *L'Osservatore Romano*, November 1, 2006.

50. See McCormick, *The Critical Calling*, p. 119.

7. Resisting the 'Dictatorship of Relativism'

1. See 'Mass "Pro Eligendo Romano Pontifice": Homily of His Eminence Card. Joseph Ratzinger, Dean of the College of Cardinals' (Vatican Basilica: Monday April 18, 2005), p. 2, accessed on February 24, 2007 at www.vatican.va/gpII/documents/homily-pro-eligendo-pontifice_20050418_en.html

2. See 'Pope Denounces Canadian Relativism' (September 8, 2006), p. 2, accessed on September 9, 2006, at www.ewtn.com/vnews/getstory.asp?number=70900

3. Joseph Cardinal Ratzinger, *Salt of the Earth: The Church at the End of the Millennium. An Interview with Peter Seewald* (San Francisco: Ignatius Press,

1997), p. 134.

4. See Joseph Ratzinger, *Values in a Time of Upheaval* (Crossroad, New York and San Francisco: Ignatius Press, 2005), pp. 53-72, at pp. 55-56; also, James Corkery, S.J., 'The Idea of Europe according to Joseph Ratzinger' in: *Milltown Studies* 31 (Spring 1993): pp. 91-111, at p. 93.

5. Joseph Cardinal Ratzinger, quoted in: 'Is It Arrogant to Say Christ is the Only Saviour? Asks Cardinal Ratzinger' (The Catholic University of St Anthony, Murcia, Spain: December. 2, 2002), at www.catholic.net/global_catholic_news/print.phtml?news_id=28413, accessed December 3, 2002.

6. Joseph Cardinal Ratzinger. *God and the World:* A Conversation with Peter Seewald (San Francisco: Ignatius Press, 2002), p. 34.

7. See Chapter 2, 'The Facial Features of a Theological *Corpus*', *supra*, pp. 28-36, at pp. 29-31.

8. *Ibid.*, see p. 30.

9. See *God and the World*, p. 34.

10. 'Is It Arrogant to Say Christ is the Only Saviour? Asks Cardinal Ratzinger,' p. 1.

11. See, for example, Ratzinger's essay 'Pluralism as a Problem for Church and Theology' in: *The Nature and Mission of Theology: Approaches to Understanding Its Role in the Light of Present Controversy* (San Francisco: Ignatius Press, 1995), pp. 73-98, at pp. 92-93. Guardini's influence on Ratzinger is decisive as regards the latter's (oft repeated) idea that, when people's philosophical presuppositions decide *a priori* – and they *do* – what can/cannot be the case, then something that is believed in Christian faith (such as, that the Absolute can – and does – enter history in the person of Jesus Christ) is deemed, in fact, incredible. It takes humility (echo: Augustine's *humilitas fidei*) to let go of such presuppositions and to open oneself to a truth that they, in principle, outlaw. Recall Augustine on the Platonists: how they sailed into the harbour of truth but refused to leave their boats, that is, they refused to bend their necks to God's flesh-taking in Jesus.

12. *Ibid.* See also Cardinal Joseph Ratzinger, 'Interreligious Dialogue and Jewish-Christian Relations,' a text prepared for a session of the *Académie des sciences morales et politiques* (Paris) and published in *Communio* 25:1 (Spring 1998): 25-40, at p. 34.

13. See Ratzinger's essay 'The Spiritual Basis and Ecclesial Identity of Theology' in *The Nature and Mission of Theology*, pp. 45-72, at p. 56. (The remark on 'metaphor' here is made also to indicate that rationality belongs to the essence of Christianity – in a way, he says [somewhat sweepingly, perhaps, in that he makes no distinction between the various kinds], that is not true of the other religions).

14. See Robert Moynihan (ed.). *Let God's Light Shine Forth: The Spiritual Vision of Pope Benedict XVI.* Part I: 'The Man and His Life,' by Robert Moynihan (London: Hutchinson, 2005) pp. 3-75, at p. 54. Moynihan dates the anti-rela-

tivism writings from 1982, but it was in the 1990s that they really flourished.

15. See 'The New Questions That Arose in the Nineties: The Position of Faith and Theology Today' in: *Truth and Tolerance: Christian Belief and World Religions* (San Francisco: Ignatius Press, 2004), pp. 115 to 137. (The original version of this text, entitled 'Relativism: The Central Problem for Faith Today', was an address delivered, in Guadalajara, Mexico, in May 1996).

16. *Dominus Jesus: On the Unicity and Salvific Universality of Jesus Christ and the Church* (Vatican: August 6, 2000); accessed at www.vatican.va on September 11, 2006.

17. *Ibid.*, see n. 4.

18. *Ibid.*, n. 5.

19. *Ibid.*, see n. 3.

20. Here the text is drawing on *Gaudium et Spes*, 22, and on n. 29 of the 1992 Instruction *Dialogue and Proclamation*; the latter is a text of the Pontifical Council for Interreligious Dialogue and the Pontifical Council for the Evangelization of Peoples. Here see also Ratzinger's 'Interreligious Dialogue and Jewish-Christian Relations,' p. 39.

21. See 'Intervento del Cardinale Prefetto Joseph Ratzinger in Occasione della Presentazione della Dichiarazione *Dominus Jesus*' alla Sala Stampa della Santa Sede,' n. 1 (accessed on September 11, 2006, at file://P:\Intervento del Cardinale Ratzinger.htm).

22. Ratzinger, 'The New Questions That Arose in the Nineties,' p. 120.

23. *Ibid.*

24. See 'Intervento del Cardinale Prefetto Joseph Ratzinger in Occasione della Presentazione della Dichiarazione *Dominus Jesus*', n. 2.

25. 'Interreligious Dialogue and Jewish-Christian Relations,' p. 38.

26. *Ibid.*, p. 39. (Note that Ratzinger is drawing here on H. Bürkle [1979] and P. Beyerhaus [1996] for 'the proper understanding of mission;' also he is drawing on the observations of his friend, Robert Spaemann, in the latter's essay 'Ist eine nicht-missionarische Praxis universalistischer Religionen möglich?,' in: *Theorie und Praxis. Festschrift N. Lobkowicz zum 65. Geburtstag* [Berlin, 1996], 41-48).

27. See 'The New Questions That Arose in the Nineties,' pp. 121-122; also 'Interreligious Dialogue and Jewish-Christian Relations', section 3 ('Greatness and Limitations of the Mystical Religions'), pp. 32-4.

28. On these anthropological points, see Chapter 3, 'On Being Human', *supra*, pp. 37-51.

29. See 'The New Questions That Arose in the Nineties,' p. 122.

30. *Ibid.*, pp. 120-121.

31. 'Interreligious Dialogue and Jewish-Christian Relations,' p. 37.

32. See *Dominus Jesus*, n. 22.

33. Gerard Hall, 'Catholic Church Teaching on Its Relationship to

Other Religions since Vatican II' in: *Australian Ejournal of Theology* 3 (February 2003), pp. 6-7.

34. *Ibid.*, p. 7.

35. *Ibid.*

36. The cardinals I refer to are Roger Mahony of Los Angeles and Edward Cassidy of Australia (then President of the Pontifical Council for Promoting Christian Unity). The archbishops are Alexander Brunett of Seattle and Rembert Weakland of Milwaukee. All but Cassidy are cited in: Peter Chirico, '*Dominus Jesus* as an Event' in: *America* (March 26, 2001): 24-28, at p. 27. Cassidy is cited (from the Italian newspaper *Corriere della Sera*) in: *America* (October 7, 2000), p. 5. (I am indebted to Hall's article for alerting me to these references.)

37. See Benedict XVI, 'Faith, Reason and the University: Memories and Reflections'. Lecture delivered to the Representatives of Science in the Aula Magna of the University of Regensburg on September 12, 2006. Accessed at www.vatican.va/holy_father/benedict_xvi/speeches/2006/september/documents/hf..., pp. 1-9, at 2 and 3.

38. *Ibid.*, see pp. 2, 3 and 4.

39. *Ibid.*, see p. 2-3 and endnote 5 on p. 8.

40. See, also, 'Christ is the Apex of the History of Salvation,' where Pope Benedict, continuing his catechesis on St Paul in his general audiences (here on September 8, 2006), highlights the absolute centrality of Christ for Paul, whose life was 'literally revolutionised' by his encounter with Jesus on the road to Damascus. 'Christ became his *raison d'etre* and the profound inspiration behind all his apostolic labours. ... In truth, Christ Jesus is the apex of the history of salvation and, hence, the true point of reference in dialogue with other religions.' Accessed at www.ewtn.com/vnews/getstory.asp?number=73145 on November 9, 2006.

41. See John F. Haught, *Mystery and Promise* (Collegeville, MN: The Liturgical Press, 1993), pp. 81-82.

42. See 'Interreligious Dialogue and Jewish-Christian Relations,' pp. 37-38.

43. *Ibid.*, p. 38.

44. See nn. 18 and 19 of *Dominus Jesus*, noting that they draw (*inter alia*) on nn. 15, 17 and 18 of Pope John Paul's 1990 Encyclical *Redemptoris Missio*.

45. See G. Hall, *art. cit.*, p. 6 (drawing on *Redemptoris Missio*, 20, and *Dialogue and Proclamation*, 35).

46. Pope John Paul II, *Redemptoris Missio*, 28 (accessed at www.vatican.va/edocs/ENG0219/_P5.HTM on June 5, 2007).

47. *Dominus Jesus*, 22, referring to Pius XII's encyclical letter *Mystici Corporis* (1943).

48. *America* (March 26, 2001): 27.

49. See Gavin D'Costa, 'Vatican II and the Status of other Religions as

Salvific Structures' in: Liam Bergin (ed.), *Faith, Word and Culture* (Dublin: The Columba Press, 2004), pp. 9-24, at 11 and 15-16.

50. *Ibid.*, p. 11.

51. See Joseph Ratzinger/Benedikt XVI, *Jesus von Nazaret. Erster Teil: Von der Taufe im Jordan bis zur Verklärung* (Freiburg, Basel, Wien: Herder Verlag, 2007), pp. 134f.

52. See Jacob Neusner, 'Renewing Religious Disputation in Quest of Theological Truth,' prepared very recently for *Communio: Internationale Katholische Zeitschrift* following the publication of Benedict XVI's book in order to shed some light on the background to Benedict's use of Neusner's *A Rabbi Talks with Jesus: An Intermillennial Interfaith Exchange* (New York: Doubleday, 1993).

53. *God and the World*, p. 34.

54. See Chapter 3, 'On Being Human', *supra*, p. 41.

55. *Salt of the Earth*, p. 133.

56. For these views of Antiseri, see his 'A Spy in the Service of the Most High', part of an essay published in the magazine of the Sacred Heart University in Milan, *Vita e Pensiero* 5:2005. Accessed, November 11, 2005, at www.chiesa.espressonline.it/printDettaglio.jsp?id=41533&eng=y

8. Europe

1. See 'Europe: Its Spiritual Foundations Today and Tomorrow' in: Joseph Cardinal Ratzinger, *Europe Today and Tomorrow: Addressing the Fundamental Issues.* Trans. Michael J. Miller (San Francisco: Ignatius Press, 2007), pp. 11-34, at p. 24. This is the third appearance of this essay, in English, in less than two years, since it was published also in two collections from 2006 that append the words 'Pope Benedict XVI' to Ratzinger's name on their title-pages. Two of the three collections carrying the essay bear the Ignatius Press imprint. It can safely be said that Ratzinger's election to the papacy has led to a veritable publishing frenzy involving a great deal of repetition, so readers take note: there is not as much to read as you may think. The other (virtually identical) reproductions of the essay cited here are 'The Spiritual Roots of Europe: Yesterday, Today, and Tomorrow' in: Joseph Ratzinger Now Pope Benedict XVI and Marcello Pera, *Without Roots: The West, Relativism, Christianity, Islam* (New York: Basic Books, 2006), pp. 51-80; and 'Europe's Identity: Its Intellectual Foundations Yesterday, Today, and Tomorrow' in: Joseph Cardinal Ratzinger (Pope Benedict XVI), *Values in a Time of Upheaval* (New York: Crossroad and San Francisco: Ignatius Press, 2006), pp. 129-150.

2. 'Europe: Its Spiritual Foundations Today and Tomorrow,' see p. 22.

3. *Ibid.*

4. *Ibid.*, see pp. 22-23.

5. See *ibid*, p. 34, also pp. 25-26; also pp. 96f. in Ratzinger's essay, 'In Search of Peace' in: *Europe Today and Tomorrow*, pp. 85-100. On contemporary Europe's seeming asymptotic approach to its own end, see 'Europe: Its Spiritual Foundations Today and Tomorrow,' pp. 22, 23 and 24; in addition, see 'Europe in the Crisis of Cultures' in: *Communio* 32 (Summer 2005): 345-356, at 353-353 and 355. Before its publication, this text was an address given at the Convent of Saint Scholastica, Subiaco, Italy, on the evening of April 1, 2005, the day before Pope John Paul II died.

6. Joseph Ratzinger, 'Europe in the Crisis of Cultures,' p. 348; see also p. 345.

7. From this time, three books of Ratzinger come to mind: *Christlicher Glaube und Europa. 12 Predigten* (Munich: Pressereferat der Erzdiözese München und Freising, no date given, but the contents date from November 1978 to April 1981); *Zeitfragen und christlicher Glaube: Acht Predigten aus den Münchner Jahren* (Würzburg, Verlag Naumann, 1982); and *Wendezeit für Europa? Diagnosen und Prognosen zur Lage von Kirche und Welt* (Einsiedeln: Johannes Verlag, 1991), published in English as *Turning-point for Europe?* (San Francisco: Ignatius Press, 1994). Three earlier essays, first published in German in 1992, are also important for the topic of Europe. They deal with truth and with the significance of moral and religious values in pluralistic democracies, and they were all reprinted in Ratzinger's collection *Values in a Time of Upheaval*. They are chapters 3, 4 and 5 of the book and are entitled, respectively, 'Freedom, Law and the Good: Moral Principles in Democratic Societies' (pp. 45-52); 'What is Truth? The Significance of Religious and Ethical Values in a Pluralistic Society' (pp. 53-72); and 'If You Want Peace…: Conscience and Truth' (pp. 75-99).

8. See James Corkery, S.J., 'The Idea of Europe according to Joseph Ratzinger' in: *Milltown Studies* 31 (Spring 1993): 91-111, at 93-97 (for a more detailed treatment than can be given in these pages).

9. *Ibid.*, see pp. 93-94, drawing on Ratzinger's essay 'Europe: A Heritage with Obligations for Christians' in his book *Church, Ecumenism and Politics: New Essays in Ecclesiology* (New York: Crossroad, 1988; original German 1979), pp. 221-236, at pp. 228-229 and p. 233. Ratzinger himself is making reference here to H. Kuhn's book, *Der Staat* (Munich, 1967), pp. 25-26, and to C. Meier's article, 'Demokratie,' in: *Geschichtliche Grundbegriffe. Historisches Lexikon zur politischsozialen Sprache in Deutschland* (Stuttgart, 1973), pp. 829f..

10. *Ibid.*, see p. 94; and see 'Europe: A Heritage with Obligations for Christians,' pp. 229-230. See also Ratzinger's essay 'Die Verantwortung des Christen für Europa' in: *Zeitfragen und christlicher Glaube*, pp. 28-32, at p. 28; and see his homily (dated 13 September 1980) 'Wahrer Friede und wahre Kultur: Christlicher Glaube und Europa' in: *Christlicher Glaube und Europa. 12 Predigten*, pp. 7-18, at pp. 8-9.

11. 'Europe: A Heritage with Obligations for Christians,' p. 230.

12. 'Wahrer Friede und wahre Kultur,' pp. 8-9; also 'Die Verantwortung des Christen für Europa,' p. 28.

13. James Corkery, 'The Idea of Europe according to Joseph Ratzinger,' p. 95. See also 'Europe: A Heritage with Obligations for Christians,' p. 234.

14. *Ibid.*, see p. 95; and see 'Europe: A Heritage with Obligations for Christians,' p. 230.

15. *Ibid.*

16. 'Europe: A Heritage with Obligations for Christians,' p. 230.

17. *Ibid.*. Notice Ratzinger's reliance, for his description of the medieval *res publica christiana*, on H. Gollwitzer, 'Europa, Abendland' in: J. Ritter (ed.), *Historisches Wörterbuch der Philosophie*, vol. II (Basle/ Stuttgart, 1972), p. 825.

18. *Ibid.*, p. 231.

19. Homily 'Wahrer Friede und wahre Kultur', p. 9.

20. 'Europe: A Heritage with Obligations for Christians,' p. 232.

21. See 'Europe in the Crisis of Cultures,' p. 354.

22. This is a constant and much-emphasised Ratzinger point. See 'Europe: A Heritage with Obligations for Christians,' p. 232. See 'Europe in the Crisis of Cultures,' especially from p. 351 onwards. Also, see 'Reflections on Europe' in: *Europe Today and Tomorrow*, pp. 35-44, at pp. 41-44.

23. See 'Europe: A Heritage with Obligations for Christians,' p. 231, also (see note 7 above) 'What is Truth? The Significance of Religious and Ethical Values in a Pluralistic Society,' p. 55.

24. 'Europe in the Crisis of Cultures,' p. 355; see also p. 350 on Europe's new identity that is defined exclusively by Enlightenment culture. On this culture's ultimate dispensing with the human being, see also p. 352. And see Ulrich Ruh, 'Joseph Ratzinger – der Kritiker der Moderne,' in: F. Meier-Hamidi and F. Schumacher (eds.), *Der Theologe Joseph Ratzinger*. Quaestiones Disputatae, no. 222 (Herder: Freiburg, 2007), pp. 119-128, at p. 124.

25. J. Ratzinger (at an evening forum at the Catholic Academy of Bavaria with Jürgen Habermas on 19 January 2004) in a talk entitled 'That Which Holds the World Together: The Pre-political Moral Foundations of a Free State' in: *Europe Today and Tomorrow*, pp. 67-81, at p. 79 (see also p. 81). And see 'Europe in the Crisis of Cultures,' section 1 ('Reflections on today's contrasting cultures'), pp. 345-350, especially pp. 348f..

26. 'Europe in the Crisis of Cultures,' p. 347.

27. *Ibid.*

28. See 'Europe in the Crisis of Cultures,' pp. 347-349. See also 'Reflections on Europe,' pp. 42-43. And see 'Europe: Its Spiritual Foundations Today and Tomorrow,' p. 23.

29. 'Europe in the Crisis of Cultures,' p. 347.

30. This form of expression is Ratzinger's; see 'Letter to Marcello Pera' in *Without Roots*, p. 133.

31. See 'Europe in the Crisis of Cultures,' pp. 348-349; also 'Europe: Its

Spiritual Foundations Today and Tomorrow,' pp. 30f. , and pp. 20-21. See also Lieven Boeve, 'Europe in Crisis: A Question of Belief or Unbelief? Perspectives from the Vatican' in: *Modern Theology* 23:2 (April 2007): 205-227, at 212-213.

32. See J. Corkery, 'The Idea of Europe according to Joseph Ratzinger,' pp. 103-105. See also 'Europe: Its Spiritual Foundations Today and Tomorrow,' p. 33.

33. See 'Europe in the Crisis of Cultures,' pp. 348-349.

34. 'Europe: Its Spiritual Foundations Today and Tomorrow,' p. 33.

35. See Joseph Ratzinger, 'Letter to Marcello Pera' in *Without Roots* (see note 1 above), p.116.

36. See 'Europe in the Crisis of Cultures,' pp. 351-353; 'In Search of Peace,' pp. 94-95; 'That Which Holds the World Together,' p. 80; 'Reflections on Europe,' p. 42; and Ulrich Ruh, 'Joseph Ratzinger – Kritiker der Moderne,' p. 124.

37. See 'Reflections on Europe,' p. 42, and 'Europe in the Crisis of Cultures,' pp. 347 and 351.

38. See 'Europe: Its Spiritual Foundations Today and Tomorrow,' p. 24.

39. See 'Europe: Its Spiritual Foundations Today and Tomorrow,' p. 33; and see Ratzinger's 2002 essay, 'Political Visions and the Praxis of Politics' in *Europe Today and Tomorrow*, pp. 47-66, at p. 65. Note how Marcello Pera picks up on Ratzinger's reference to how freedom of speech becomes the supreme good only when it comes to Jesus Christ and what is sacred to Christians (see 'Letter from Marcello Pera to Joseph Ratzinger' in *Without Roots*, pp. 81-106, at p. 89).

40. See 'Europe in the Crisis of Cultures,' pp. 349-350; also p. 351 and pp. 352-353.

41. See 'Letter to Marcello Pera,' p. 128.

42. See Lieven Boeve, 'Europe in Crisis,' pp. 208, 211, 213.

43. See 'Europe in the Crisis of Cultures,' pp. 351-352, also pp. 349-350.

44. See Joseph Ratzinger, 'Faith in the Triune God, and Peace in the World,' in: *Europe Today and Tomorrow*, pp. 101-107, at 102-103.

45. See 'Europe: Its Spiritual Foundations Today and Tomorrow,' p. 34; and 'Letter to Marcello Pera,' pp. 120-123, and 126.

46. 'Europe in the Crisis of Cultures,' p. 348.

47. *Ibid.*, see pp. 354-355. See also Marcello Pera's 'Introduction: A Proposal That Should be Accepted', pp. 7-22, in yet another collection of Joseph Ratzinger's speeches/writings that have been published since he became Pope Benedict XVI: *Christianity and the Crisis of Cultures* (San Francisco: Ignatius Press, 2006). Also, see 'Reflections on Europe,' pp. 43-44, and p. 34.

48. See J. Corkery, 'The Idea of Europe according to Joseph Ratzinger,', pp. 92-93; also, see 'Europe: Its Spiritual Foundations Today, and Tomorrow,' p.

11, where Ratzinger says: 'Europe is not a continent that can be comprehended neatly in geographical terms; rather it is a cultural and historical concept.'

49. See 'Europe: Its Spiritual Foundations Today and Tomorrow'. This title does not suggest a search for Europe's identity through examining its past, but the titles borne by the other two versions of it that were referred to earlier (see footnote 1 above) do, for they each mention Europe's 'Yesterday.' Also, see the remarks of Ratzinger himself in his 'Preface' to *Europe Today and Tomorrow*, pp. 7-8, at p. 7.

50. Preface to *Europe Today and Tomorrow*, p. 7.

51. Tracey Rowland, *Ratzinger's Faith: The Theology of Pope Benedict XVI* (Oxford: Oxford University Press, 2008), p. 122.

52. See 'Europe in the Crisis of Cultures,' p. 355; also p. 353.

53. *Ibid.*, see p. 346.

54. He says it cannot be denied that the 'cultures' of Christian faith and Western secular rationality are the two main partners in today's intercultural context (see 'That Which Holds the World Together,' p. 81).

55. 'In Search of Peace,' pp. 96-97.

56. *Ibid.*, p. 97.

57. See J. Ratzinger, 'The Right to Life,' in: *Christianity and the Crisis of Cultures*, pp. 55-73, at p. 71. See also note 44 above.

58. See 'Letter to Marcello Pera,' pp. 125-126.

59. *Ibid.*, see p. 127.

60. See 'Europe in the Crisis of Cultures,' p. 355.

61. See: 'Europe in the Crisis of Cultures,' especially pp. 348-350 and p. 352; 'Europe: Its Spiritual Foundations Today and Tomorrow,' especially pp. 20-21, 30-31; 'Reflections on Europe,' pp. 42-43.

62. See 'Communication and Culture: New Methods of Evangelization in the Third Millennium' in: Joseph Ratzinger, *On the Way to Jesus Christ* (San Francisco: Ignatius Press, 2005), pp. 42-52, at 46-48.

63. See Werner G. Jeanrond, 'The Future of Christianity in Europe' in: W. G. Jeanrond and Andrew D. H. Mayes, eds., *Recognising the Margins: Developments in Biblical and Theological Studies. Essays in Honour of Seán Freyne* (Dublin: The Columba Press, 2006), pp. 182-200, at pp. 185-189 especially.

64. *Ibid.*, p. 184.

65. *Ibid.*, p. 189.

66. *Ibid.*, p. 190; on his caution about 'identity' language, see also pp. 185-6f., 189, 190-191, 199-200.

67. *Ibid.*, see pp. 192-193.

68. Gillian Wylie, 'Fostering a Union of Permanent Contrasts: A Case for Turkish Membership of the European Union' in: Jesuit Centre for Faith and Justice, *The Future of Europe: Uniting Vision, Values and Citizens?* (Dublin: Veritas, 2006), pp. 46-56, at p. 52. (For evidence that Ratzinger is not far from her thoughts, see p. 47).

69. 'Europe: Its Spiritual Foundations Today and Tomorrow,' p. 11 (and note 48 above).

70. Jeanrond, 'The Future of Christianity in Europe,' see pp. 188-189; also p. 185.

71. *Ibid., passim.*, especially pp. 185-189 and 193-199.

72. *Ibid.*, see pp. 194-199.

73. *Ibid.*, p. 192; see also pp. 186f.

74. See Bernice Martin, 'Hold the Fort' in *Times Literary Supplement* (March 2007). Martin is reviewing *Without Roots: The West, Relativism, Christianity, Islam* by Joseph Ratzinger and Marcello Pera.

75. *Ibid.*

76. J. Ratzinger, 'The Grace of Reconciliation,' in: *Europe Today and Tomorrow*, pp. 114-117, at 116-'7.

77. See 'Europe and the Crisis of Cultures,' p. 348.

78. *Ibid.*, see p. 347.

79. *Ibid.*

80. Recall Ratzinger's 1980 homily 'Wahrer Friede und wahre Kultur: Christlicher Glaube und Europe': 'Europe became Europe through the Christian faith, which carries within it the heritage of Israel but has, at the same time, taken to itself (assimilated) the best of the Greek and Roman spirit.'

81. Tracey Rowland, *Ratzinger's Faith*, p. 111. She goes on to quote these words from *Fides et Ratio* (one cannot help wondering if the then Prefect of the Congregation for the Doctrine of the Faith, Cardinal Ratzinger, had a hand in drafting them): 'In engaging great cultures for the first time the Church cannot abandon what she has gained from her inculturation in the world of Greco-Latin thought. To reject this heritage would be to deny the providential plan of God who guides his Church down the paths of time and history.'

82. See previous footnote.

83. See *Europe Today and Tomorrow* (various essays), pp. 63-64, 80-81, 87, 91-100 (especially pp. 93-96).

84. 'Wahrer Friede und wahre Kultur,' p. 9; and see note 19 above.

85. 'A Christian Orientation in a Pluralistic Democracy,' p. 230.

9. Wise Cautions and Legitimate Hopes

1. For example, I could have offered separate treatments of the Church, and of eschatology, although I console myself that others have done so; even in English work is beginning to appear in these areas.

2. Joseph Cardinal Ratzinger with Vittorio Messori, *The Ratzinger Report: An Exclusive Interview on the State of the Church* (San Francisco: Ignatius Press, 1985), p. 35. See also pp. 31 and 113.

3. *Ibid.*, see pp. 34-35.

4. Joseph Cardinal Ratzinger, 'Church and World: An Inquiry into the Reception of Vatican Council II' in: *Principles of Catholic Theology: Building Stones for a Fundamental Theology* (San Francisco: Ignatius Press, 1987, orginal German 1982, with the text that I'm referring to dating from 1975), pp. 378-393, at p. 390.

5. See *ibid.*, also *The Ratzinger Report*, p. 40.

6. *The Ratzinger Report*, p. 40.

7. See *ibid.*, pp. 31, 34, 37 and 40; and see 'Church and World', p. 390.

8. Pope Benedict XVI, 'Christmas, the Council and Conversion in Christ' in: *L'Osservatore Romano*. Weekly English Edition, 4 January 2006, pp. 4-6, at p. 5.

9. *Ibid.*

10. *Ibid.*

11. *Ibid.*

12. John Paul II at a conference held in the Vatican in 2000. Quoted in John W. O'Malley, S.J., 'Vatican II: Did Anything Happen?' in: *Theological Studies* 67 (2006): 3-33, at p. 5. O'Malley's source for the Pope's words is Sandro Magister, 'Vatican II: The Real Untold Story', 27 July 2005, at http://www.chiesa.espressonline.it/dettaglio.jsp?id=34283&eng=y accessed by O'Malley on October 31, 2005

13. Giuseppe Alberigo (General Editor) and Joseph A. Komonchak (editor of English version), *History of Vatican II*. Five volumes (Leuven, Belgium: Peeters and Maryknoll, NY: Orbis, 1995-2006).

14. John W. O'Malley, *art. cit.*, p. 4.

15. *Ibid.*, see pp. 4-5.

16. John W. O'Malley's 'Vatican II: Did Anything Happen?' is one clear example; so also is Alberigo's book, *A Brief History of Vatican II* (Maryknoll, New York: Orbis Books, 2006). And the recent appearance of O'Malley's book, *What Happened at Vatican II*, is further evidence that Ruini is engaged in wishful thinking (see Introduction, *supra*, p. 15).

17. See John W. O'Malley, 'Vatican II: A Matter of Style' in: *2003 President's Letter*, Weston Jesuit School of Theology (Cambridge, MA: Weston Jesuit School of Theology, 2003).

18. See O'Malley, 'Vatican II: Did Anything Happen?,' pp. 19-20.

19. See Giuseppe Alberigo, *A Brief History of Vatican II*, chapter 1, pp. 1-4 ('A Surprise Announcement'), pp. 9-10 ('What Kind of Council?'), and pp. 18-20 ('Preparation for What Sort of Council?').

20. See John W. O'Malley, 'Vatican II: Did Anything Happen?,' pp. 27-31; also p. 17. See his 'Vatican II: A Matter of Style,' pp. 3-5 especially.

21. Alberigo frequently stresses Vatican II's continuity with Catholic tradition; however, as O'Malley points out in his *Foreword* to Alberigo's *A Brief History*, Alberigo's underscoring of Vatican II's basic continuity with the

Catholic tradition does not blind him to the fact that the Council also wanted to do something more (see Foreword, pp. vii-viii, at p. viii).

22. 'Vatican II: Did Anything Happen?,' p. 29.

23. *Ibid.*, see p. 31.

24. *Ibid.*, p. 33.

25. See 'Christmas, the Council and Conversion in Christ,' pp. 5-6. Also, see Jared Wicks, S.J., 'Review Article: New Light on Vatican Council II' in: *The Catholic Historical Review* XCII:4 (October 2006), pp. 609-628, at pp. 613-614.

26. *Ibid.*, see p. 613; see O'Malley, pp. 4-5 (on Marchetto's and Ruini's views) and p. 6 (on Alberigo's).

27. These circles of questions were, according to Benedict, the relationship between faith and modern science; the relationship between the Church and the modern State; and the relationship between Christian faith and world religions.

28. 'Christmas, the Council and Conversion in Christ,' p. 6.

29. *Ibid.*

30. Avery Cardinal Dulles, 'From Ratzinger to Benedict,' in: *First Things* (February 2006). Note how, towards the end of his article, Dulles writes: 'Ratzinger's career appears to have affected his theology.'

31. See 'First Homily as Pope' in: Robert Moynihan (ed.), *The Spiritual Vision of Pope Benedict XVI* (London: Hutchinson, 2005), pp. 188-197, at p. 191. (This was in fact the new Pope's inauguration homily; his first homily as Pope was to the College of Cardinals the day after he was elected).

32. See Raphael Gallagher, C.Ss.R., 'The Practice of Love by the Church. Part 2 of *Deus Caritas Est*,' in: *Studia Moralia* 45/1 (Gennaio-Giugno 2007): 29-40, at p. 31.

33. *Ibid.*, footnote 9.

34. *Ibid.*, p. 31.

35. *Ibid.*, see pp. 39-40.

36. Benedict XVI, Homily to the College of Cardinals on April 20, 2005. Text quoted from Matthew E. Bunson, *We Have a Pope! Benedict XVI* (Huntington, IN: Our Sunday Visitor Publishing Division, Our Sunday Visitor, Inc., 2005), pp. 100-106, at p. 102.

37. Gallagher, *art. cit.*, p. 38; also p. 31.

38. *Ibid.*, see pp. 32-33; also p. 39.

39. See Basilio Petrà, '*Deus Caritas Est*: A Thematic and Conceptual Analysis of Part One' in: *Studia Moralia* 45 (2007): 11-28, at 25. (Note also Raphael Gallagher speaking of justice being conceived as the consequence of love in *Deus Caritas Est*).

40. See Gallagher, *art. cit.*, pp. 32-33.

41. See article by Sandro Magister, 'Benedict XVI, Live. Fifteen Questions, and as Many Responses', March 7, 2006, accessed at http://chiesa.

espresso.repubblica.it/articolo/46491?&eng=y on October 1, 2007.

42. Avery Dulles, 'From Ratzinger to Benedict,' pp. 3-4.

43. David Gibson, *The Rule of Benedict: Pope Benedict XVI and His Battle with the Modern World* (USA: HarperSanFrancisco, 2006), p. 216.

44. *Ibid.*

45. See *The Ratzinger Report*, p. 18.

46. See John Jay Hughes, 'Liberated by the Papacy? Two Books about a Pope with Gravitas,' in: *America* (August 15-22, 2005): 22-24, at 24.

47. See Sandro Magister, 'Benedict XVI, a Pope Armed with "Purity",' at http://chiesa.espresso.repubblica.it/articolo/103921?&eng=y, accessed on October 1, 2007

48. See 'Interview with Benedict XVI (Part 2),' at www.catholic.org/printer_friendly.php?id=3571&section=Featured+Today, p. 7. Interview conducted on August 5 and accessed on August 21, 2006,

49. See James Corkery, *The Relationship Between Human Existence and Christian Salvation in the Theology of Joseph Ratzinger* (Ann Arbor, MI: University Microfilms International), 1991, pp. 494-500.

50. Avery Dulles, 'From Ratzinger to Benedict,' final page.

51. See David Gibson, *The Rule of Benedict*, pp. 251-252.

52. See 'Benedikt XVI: Wegweisung für die Kirche Lateinamerikas' in *Herder Korrespondenz* 61 (6/2007), 277-279 (the article is signed by U.R.).

53. Interview with Cardinal Hummes, 'Unlikely Bureaucrat' in: *The Tablet* (12 May 2007): 12-13, at 12.

54. 'Benedikt XVI: Wegweisung für die Kirche Lateinamerikas,' p. 279.

55. Paul Elie, 'The Year of the Two Popes: How Joseph Ratzinger Stepped into the Shoes of John Paul II – and What It Means for the Catholic Church,' *The Atlantic Monthly* (January-February 2006): 64-92, at 91.

56. David Gibson, *The Rule of Benedict*, p. 248.

57. The CDF text: *Responses to Some Questions Regarding Certain Aspects of the Doctrine on the Church*, accessed at http://www.vatican.va/roman_curia/congregations/cfaith/documents/rc_con_cfaith_doc_ on July 10, 2007; on Cardinal Lehmann's remarks, see Christa Pongratz-Lippitt, 'Cardinal Criticises "One True Church" Document,' in: *The Tablet* (6 October 2007): 29.

58. See Thomas Söding, 'Aufklärung über Jesus. Das Jesus-Buch des Papstes und das Programm seines Pontifikates,' in: *Herder Korrespondenz* 61 (6/2007): 281-285, at 282.

59. See 'Interview with Benedict XVI (Part 2),' p. 4.

60. See André Lascaris, O.P., 'A Church without the Eucharist?: Dutch Catholics Looking at the Future', *Doctrine & Life*, vol. 57, no. 3, March 2007, pp. 46-50.

61. See David Gibson, *The Rule of Benedict*, p. 216.

62. Paul Elie, *art. cit.*, p. 91 (see 91-92). The words 'so far' refer roughly

to Benedict's first nine months, but this pattern has continued.

63. This title was given to an article of mine in *The Catholic Herald* (London), 3 February 2006, p. 15.

64. See Sandro Magister, 'Benedict XVI, a Pope Armed with "Purity",' p. 2. See also Gibson, p. 241.

65. See 'Interview with Benedict XVI (Part 1),' p. 5.

66. See Drew Christiansen, 'Benedict XVI: Peacemaker' in: *America* (July 16-23, 2007): 10-15.

67. David Gibson, *The Coming Catholic Church: How the Faithful Are Shaping a New American Catholicism* (HarperSanFrancisco, 2003), p. 322.